MARRIAGE

I first met my wife in the Tunnel of Love.
She was digging it.

•

LOVE

Marie: Am I the first girl you've ever made love to?

Tam: Possibly. Were you behind the aircraft hangar at Glasgow Airport in December, 1959?

•

RELIGION

I passed our vicar the other day. 'Hello Father,' I greeted him. 'Still on a one day week?'

•

THE SCOTS

What is a Scot? I keep getting asked that. He's a man who keeps the Sabbath – and everything else he can lay his hands on.

•

MEDICINE

Patient: Doctor, I've got three minutes to live. Can you do anything for me?

Doctor: I could boil you an egg.

•

EDUCATION

Teacher: Where's Uganda?

Wee Boy: Buried next to my Grandma.

•

POLITICS

Helen: What do you think of Red China?

Bella: It's nice on a white tablecloth.

Andrew Yule lives in Kilmarnock, Scotland. He is the author of *Hollywood A-Go-Go, David Puttnam: The Story So Far,* and *The Best Way to Walk: The Chic Murray Story.*

Also by Andrew Yule
THE BEST WAY TO WALK: THE CHIC MURRAY STORY
and published by Corgi Books

The Best Way to Laugh

THE CHIC MURRAY
BUMPER FUN BOOK

Compiled and Edited by
Andrew Yule

CORGI BOOKS

THE BEST WAY TO LAUGH: THE CHIC MURRAY
BUMPER FUN BOOK
A CORGI BOOK 0 552 13854 1

First publication in Great Britain

PRINTING HISTORY
Corgi edition published 1991

This book is set in 10/11½pt Palatino by
Kestrel Data, Exeter

Corgi Books are published by Transworld Publishers Ltd.,
61-63 Uxbridge Road, Ealing, London W5 5SA, in Australia
by Transworld Publishers (Australia) Pty. Ltd., 15-23 Helles
Avenue, Moorebank, NSW 2170, and in New Zealand by
Transworld Publishers (N.Z.) Ltd., Cnr. Moselle and
Waipareira Avenues, Henderson, Auckland.

Made and printed in Great Britain by
Cox & Wyman Ltd., Reading, Berks.

For Maidie Murray

CONTENTS

INTRODUCTION

With *The Best Way To Walk, THE CHIC MURRAY STORY* high in the Scottish best-selling lists, I asked Maidie Murray out for a celebratory dinner. Over a couple of frozen margaritas we looked back at the fun we'd had going through Chic's old scripts and notes. Over their years together as Chic and Maidie – the Tall Droll with the Small Doll, as they were billed in variety throughout the length and breadth of Britain – Maidie had proved a veritable magpie, hoarding all their reviews, programmes and contracts, material that proved invaluable in the writing of *The Best Way To Walk*.

At my mention of 'magpie' over dinner, Maidie smiled. 'I wasn't the only one,' she pointed out. 'Chic used to make a note every time he thought of a funny line or phrase. Even if he heard one line out of a half-hour radio programme that tickled his fancy, down it would go in the mass of notes he always kept.' There were, it seemed, a couple of suitcases still unexplored.

A few days later Maidie phoned me. Would I care to attend the ceremonial opening of these suitcases? Neither of us was prepared for the dozens of school jotters, letter pads and sheaves of correspondence that were inside – all of them covered with Chic's distinctive, often almost illegible scrawl. I spent hours that day, as well as the next few months, poring over the material.

9

There were the beginning of jokes, the middle of jokes, the end of jokes – then, bliss, a complete 'tale' from Chic. There were funny stories that had tickled Chic's fancy, both fresh and borrowed, hilarious letters and postcards, together with invaluable original material by the master of mirth himself that had me in fits of laughter. Sifting through the precious pages was like being on an archaeological dig. The unexpected riches included a whole series of spoof movies Chic had planned to 'produce', while some of the scribbled notes reminded Maidie of incidents in their life together she had all but forgotten.

The Chic Murray Bumper Fun Book was the name that immediately suggested itself for the collection. Just as Chic had found 'The Best Way To Walk' in his lifetime, so he had left us a sidesplitting legacy of 'The Best Way To Laugh'.

ANDREW YULE

1

HOME SWEET HOME

In many ways I had a wonderful family life as a child. We could have been featured on *Happy Families* any time. I don't think my parents liked me to begin with, though. They made me wear a label around my neck with someone else's address on it. The worst day was when they sent me out to play and when I got back, they'd moved.

But there's no trace of insanity in our family. Oh no, we all had baths every day. Me and my three sisters had endless fun and games as children, mainly playing snakes and ladders on my granny's varicose veins. My cousin had a shape like Marilyn Monroe. It was very embarrassing, since he was a boy.

My grandfather was a stuntman in Hollywood, so we never saw much of him. With one foot on each horse he did fine, until he came to a fork in the road one day. Now we see even less of him.

My parents were wonderful, always there with a ready compromise. My sister wanted a cat for a pet, I wanted a dog. They bought a cat and taught it to bark.

My dad kept a scrapbook; in it he recalled all the fights he had with my mother. Since he ate like a horse, the nosebag my mum got him was a great improvement. He was so fat he must have been born when meat was really cheap. He was a very religious man, though. He collected all of Frankie Laine's records. He would walk me to school every morning. It was handy, him being in the same class. When he got a job he used to say he was in the meat-packing business – he worked in a corset manufacturers. One thing about our family – there were no favourites. Dad hated the lot of us!

When jobs were plentiful we ate like kings. One Christmas our turkey was so big we'd to get an upholsterer to stuff it. When things were not so good I heard my mother say to a neighbour, 'I can't blether all day. I'd better get a crust on that pie before my man comes home and sees what's in it.'

One day, at what was probably our lowest ebb, mother announced there was good news and bad news. 'The bad news,' she declared, 'is that there's only pigswill for dinner. The good news – there isn't enough to go around.'

The ultimate luxury in our house at that time was ashtrays without advertisements. It was all the wolf could do to keep us away from his door. We dreamt of the day we could paper behind the cuckoo clock. We didn't have to bother with carpets. We had wall-to-wall mildew. It was the only house I've ever known with guttering inside. A luxury meal was prairie sandwiches – two hunks of bread with wide open spaces in between. We were so poor for a while we even had to drink skimmed water. There were so many holes in my socks I could put them on seventeen different ways.

I'll never forget my mother. She was just like a brother to me. I always held the door open for her when she went out to do her paper round. She was so houseproud that when my dad got up at night to sleepwalk she had the bed made by the time he got back. When a cigarette commercial came on the telly she put an ashtray under the set. She dusted everything, even the tropical fish.

My sisters were brought up very strictly. They weren't allowed to turn the cat over until they were thirteen. They've made up for it since. One of my sisters has been married so often she's bought a drip-dry wedding dress. Another has five children. 'Why don't you marry the father?' I keep asking her. 'I don't like him,' she tells me.

2

CARRY ON CHORTLING

A father told his son that he dug up the new baby under the gooseberry bush in the garden. The following day he saw the lad with muddy boots and a dirty spade. 'Have you been digging for another baby?' he asked. 'No,' the wee boy replied. 'I've been putting the other one back.'

•

This woman bought two budgies and arrived back at the pet shop a few days later. 'I can't tell the male from the female,' she complained.

'Get two worms,' the assistant suggested, 'and whichever one eats the male worm is the male bird.'

'But how can I tell which is the male worm?' she asked.

'Madam, this is a bird shop,' he told her, 'not a worm shop.'

•

After two kids had been playing together in the yard, one of them came rushing into the house. 'Mummy,' he asked. 'Can you take an appendix out if you're not a doctor?'

'Of course not.'

The child rushed back into the yard yelling, 'Jimmy, put it back'.

●

A friend of mine is a one-armed sculptor. He sticks his chisel in his mouth and hits himself over the back of his head with a hammer.

●

Beanie said she'd do anything for a fur coat. Unfortunately, by the time she got it she couldn't get it buttoned.

●

I had a tragic childhood. My parents never understood me. They were Japanese.

●

I went into Fraser's store in Princes Street last week and held them up with a price gun. 'Give me all the money in your till,' I told the girl, 'or I'll mark down everything in the store.'

●

In Spain this year I stayed in a special hotel. It was finished.

●

I always invite short guests to my parties. They make the cocktails seem bigger.

●

He was a terribly mixed-up fellow. He had Dolly Parton for a mother and was bottle-fed.

●

I'm so nervous about drowning I even wear water wings in the shower.

•

My brother-in-law's a man who can liven up any party. Providing he stays away, that is.

•

The union decided to act on a show of hands, but stipulated that everyone had to be blindfolded first.

•

I always regarded *The Times* as a quality newspaper. When you wrap fish and chips in it the vinegar never seeps through.

•

I've got a dog called Bentley. It's probably the only Bentley I'll ever own.

•

I assured my wife that I'd travel through fire, flood and pub to be with her.

•

At the moment I'm living outside of Glasgow. If I behave myself, they're going to let me in.

•

A neighbour put his budgerigar in the mincing machine and invented shredded tweet.

•

Did you notice that kitchen-sink dramas seem to have gone down the drain?

●

There was an old actor who was given a part, a very small part. All he had to say was 'it is'. He went on for weeks rehearsing 'It is, it is' and when the time came said 'Is it?' instead.

'You silly old fool,' the producer yelled. 'You've ruined the whole play.'

'Listen, laddie,' the oldster replied, 'I know my part backwards.'

●

A pal of mine's an Irish cat burglar. He's stolen fifteen cats already this week.

●

When she was a landgirl in the wheatfields our Nellie was forever working against the grain.

●

A group of children were travelling by train. All of them were herded along the corridor by the teacher, except one little lad who seemed to be lingering behind. 'Get moving,' said the teacher, 'or I'll fetch you a clip on the ear.'

'Please yourself, lady,' the 'lad' replied, 'but I'm a jockey from Musselburgh.'

●

Two of my girlfriends had a duel over me to see who would get me. One of them got me in the leg, the other got me in the arm.

●

She'd been married five times, he six. 'Be sure to show up on time,' their wedding invitation warned, 'this is no amateur affair.'

•

Fifty-five per cent of men in Toulouse wear their trousers too long, forty-five per cent of men in Toulon wear their trousers too loose.

•

I admit to spending a fortune on women, booze and gambling. The rest I spend foolishly.

•

Just a thought: are Roman Catholics allowed to eat French lettuce?

•

There's many a joke told in Glasgow that they won't laugh at in London. You know why? They can't hear it.

•

This fellow I know had tried one dandruff treatment after another without success. Then he discovered his ceiling was flaking.

•

Two spoonfuls of strawberry jam is a great cure for seasickness. And it's the only thing that tastes the same going down as it does coming up.

•

Paddy phoned the headquarters of Interpol and asked them to send his mother a dozen roses for her birthday.

•

Sentenced to ninety-nine years, the prisoner said, 'I'm seventy now, your honour, I doubt if I'll be able to serve the full term.'

'Oh, well,' the judge replied, 'just do as long as you can.'

3

MEMORIES OF INVERKIP

Inverkip is so rough they put a date stamp on your head when they mug you so they don't do you twice in the one day. My father told me one day he was going to talk to me about the vultures and locusts. I said, 'Don't you mean the birds and bees?' 'No,' he replied, 'I mean the vultures and locusts. This is *Inverkip*, lad!'

At our Indian restaurant the curries come in three strengths – strong, extremely strong, and Gandhi's Revenge.

The town's so tough some friends of mine robbed a bank and got mugged on the way to their car. It's the only place I know where the fire brigade is ex-directory.

At our local Woolworth's they weigh you coming in and going out. If you haven't bought anything and you're heavier they send you to the police station. If you weigh the same they send you to a psychiatrist.

I remember my mother was on the quayside with me. 'Someone has to fight, Mother,' I told her. 'That's right, son,' she replied. Her boat sailed within the hour.

One Inverkip worthy who'd been a riveter all his days in the yards was on his deathbed. 'You'll get a thousand, Rob, when I go,' he told his eldest son. 'And there's a thousand for Bob and Nellie as well. As for Bessie, my beloved wife, there's 10,000 for her.' They all thought he was talking in pounds – it turned out he meant rivets.

When he later announced he felt much better, his wife was furious. 'Too late!' she told him. 'I've just bought two pounds of boiled ham for the mourners.'

Two of our nudists refused to go near the sun for a year. They wanted a white wedding. I don't know which was loudest at the reception – the band or their suits.

Tam the Bam took a bodybuilding course because he was only 9 stone and 10-stone men pinched his beer. He came back from the course weighing a magnificent 13 stone. Now 14-stone men pinch his beer.

I played our local cinema manager at cards and beat him hands down. He'd completely forgotten what a full house looked like.

After one of the players collapsed at the card table in the middle of a game recently, one of his friends said, 'This is terrible. What'll we do if he dies?'

'We'll finish the game standing up,' another replied. 'As a token of respect.'

The toughest question in the local Mastermind contest: What was the colour of Dick Turpin's horse Black Bess?

If you gave a girl a bunch of flowers in Inverkip, she was regarded as having lost her amateur status. And you were regarded as engaged.

'Who killed Charles the Second?' a teacher asked one of the class at Inverkip Academy.

'I'm sorry miss, I can't tell you,' the boy replied.

'Why not?' asked the teacher.

'Because I don't like squealers,' he said.

My life of crime was brief. I went into the post office with a scarf around my neck and a gun in my hand. Then I tripped and smashed my face on the counter. The postmistress said, 'Is this a hold-up?'

I said, 'No, more like a cock-up. Give me a fivepenny stamp!'

4

IT'S A CRAZY WORLD

The audience in the theatre were glued to their seats. The manager reckoned that was the only way to keep them in.

•

Did you hear the one about the trapeze artist who caught his wife in the act? The contortionist was in dead trouble!

Or the cannonball artist who was shot into the sky and became a star overnight?

Or the one about the flea circus that started from scratch?

•

'Any coppers around here?' he asked me. When I said no, he hit me on the head and ran off with my wallet.

•

I knew a girl with a pimply face who won a spot prize at the dance.

•

'I do bird imitations,' Robin told the agent.

'We've got plenty of them,' he replied. 'We

don't need any more.' So Robin flew out the window.

●

My wife's dumpling went down the wrong way. Into my stomach.

●

Two grams of ink and Fred was blotto.

●

Sammy's not much of a ventriloquist. He speaks his lines while his dummy drinks a glass of water.

●

I hear that Britt Ekland's starting a new youth employment scheme. Apparently the opportunities are unlimited.

●

My new girlfriend told me she's got mirrors on the wall and mirrors on the bedroom ceiling. When she asked me to call she said to bring a bottle. So I brought a bottle of window cleaner.

●

When you drink Jock Reid's Special Reserve Whisky you don't wake up in the morning with a hangover. You get one the same night.

●

My ex-girlfriend's a redhead. No hair, just a red head.

●

We had a very successful membership drive at our

golf club last week. We managed to drive out thirty members.

•

My sister keeps pigeons. It's not the expense that worries her, it's the overheads.

•

I saw this rather fat girl the other day and said, 'What are you doing way out here? And here, and here, and here?'

•

When the trombone player's wig fell into his instrument he spent the entire morning blowing his top.

•

If you want to know how a cow feels when it's being milked, go along to your local income tax office.

•

An American saw Union Jacks for sale. 'How cute,' he said. 'Give me six. And do they come in any other colours?'

•

I dreamt I was forced to eat 25 lbs of marsh-mallow. When I woke up this morning, my pillow was missing.

•

My wife's had so many accidents on the road that she's painted one side of her car red and the other blue, so that witnesses will contradict each other in future.

•

There's more nutrition in a Barlinnie Prison sausage than in one and a half pounds of pulped cardboard. Both taste the same, though.

•

When Liam's gang told him to lie low, he cut the legs off his bed.

•

Our closing-down sale's been such a success, we're opening up again on Monday.

•

Len's even teeth parted in a smile. His odd ones stayed where they were.

•

Here's some good news for the small farmer: a new breed of small cows.

•

When I told my girlfriend to slip into something cool, she stepped into the fridge.

•

Maggie Thatcher is to politics what piles are to Lester Piggott. Her motto is, 'When you've got them by the balls, their hearts and minds will follow'.

•

In the Saraha Desert I asked an Arab how far it was to the sea. 'Two thousand miles,' he replied. I told him I'd stay on the beach.

•

It only rained twice during my week's holiday in Blackpool, once for three days and once for four days.

•

They caught me kissing a distant cousin. I told them I was just trying to shorten the distance.

•

I was dancing with my girlfriend and mentioned it was a nice floor. She said, 'Why don't you get off my feet and try it then?'

•

'Always wash your legs before meals,' was Mavis's motto. 'You never know who's under the table.'

•

Matty's impression of Mrs Thatcher is so good she's been beaten up six times this month already.

•

Are tall detectives paid by the yard?

•

Did you hear the one about the bald-headed Indian who married a squaw to keep his wigwam warm?

•

They're building an aquarium with special blinds for shy fish.

•

A friend of mine followed the tall dark-haired girl

for hours. Then he discovered she was a Grenadier Guard.

•

For a while there was a craze in Ireland to emigrate to China to work in the paddy fields.

•

Tommy Docherty's proud boast is that he's had more clubs than Jack Nicklaus.

5

SOMETHING
TO OFFEND EVERYONE – I
by Lil Sister

Two nuns were climbing over a convent wall at 3 a.m. in the morning. One of them turned to the other. 'You know,' she said. 'I feel like a commando.'

'So do I,' her companion replied, 'but where the hell are we going to get one at this time of the morning?'

•

A Mother Superior arose one morning and as she walked through the convent to the breakfast room, a passing nun in the corridor said, 'Good morning, Reverend Mother, I see you got up on the wrong side of the bed this morning'.

She was puzzled by this but let it pass. A few moments later another nun approached her. 'Good morning, Reverend Mother,' she said, 'I see you got up on the wrong side of the bed this morning.'

When she was just outside the dining room a third nun looked at her and said, 'Good morning, Reverend Mother, I see you got up on the wrong side of the bed this morning'.

This really stopped the Mother Superior in her

tracks. 'Listen, Sister,' she said, 'you're the third one this morning to say that. Can you tell me why?'

'Yes, Reverend Mother,' the nun replied. 'You have Father Murphy's boots on.'

•

Three pregnant nuns were dragged before the Mother Superior. 'I hope all three of you realize this is a very serious offence. And you must die for it in the manner of the father's occupation!'

She turned to the first nun: 'What was your child's father's occupation?'

'A fireman, Reverend Mother,' the nun replied.

'Well, you will be burned to death,' the Mother Superior said. 'Take her away!'

She turned to the second nun: 'What was the occupation of your child's father?'

'A bricklayer, Reverend Mother.'

'Very well, you will be stoned to death. Take her away!'

She was surprised to find the third nun laughing fit to burst. 'Sister, this is a very serious business,' she declared.

'I know it is, Reverend Mother,' the nun replied, still giggling.

'Very well,' said the Mother Superior. 'What was the occupation of your child's father?'

'A jockey, Reverend Mother,' the nun replied.

•

A nun had been out with a can collecting for charity and she ended up in a pub, where she made another collection. Afterwards she went up to the bar, whipped out a fiver and asked for a glass of vodka and a Carlsberg lager. The barman was surprised, but served her. Two hours, six glasses of vodka and three Carlsbergs later the barman decided he had to speak to her. 'Listen, you're the first nun I've ever seen drinking,' he said. 'I'm not objecting, I'm just wondering why.'

'Well, it's a cure for constipation,' the nun told him.

'Oh, I see,' the barman replied. 'You're needing to go to the toilet.'

'No, it's the Mother Superior of our convent who's constipated,' the nun explained. 'But when she gets a load of me it'll certainly cure her!'

•

A priest and a nun rode together on a camel across the desert towards their mission, hundreds of miles from civilization. Unfortunately their camel dropped dead of sunstroke. For two days the two of them lay dying of heat, hunger and thirst, with no sign of a rescue. Towards the end the priest looked at the nun. 'Well, sister,' he said, 'it seems like everything is going to be over. We'd better hear each other's confession.'

After this was done the priest turned to the nun. 'You know, Sister, the end is very near. And I've never seen a woman in the nude. Would you strip for me?'

'Certainly,' said the nun.

When she had removed her habit the priest looked at her admiringly. 'My, what a beautiful piece of God's handiwork,' he said.

'Thank you,' she replied. 'You know, Father, I've never seen a man in the nude either. Would you mind stripping for me?'

'Certainly,' said the priest.

With his cassock removed, the nun looked at him admiringly. 'My, what a beautiful body,' she declared. 'But what's that between your legs?'

'That's a gift straight from God. It's the giver of life,' said the priest.

'Well,' said the nun, 'I wish you'd use it to activate that dead camel so we can get the hell out of here.'

•

A motorist drove frantically into the city zoo and asked the head keeper, 'What's the average height of penguins?'

'Two to three feet tall, sir.'

'My God,' said the motorist. 'I've knocked down two nuns!'

6

CHIC'S CORRESPONDENCE FILE

A letter to the RAC Club, London:

'Dear Sirs,

What is going on? I have been a member of your organization for a fortnight already and so far have received only a badge. Where is the rest of my uniform? Kindly despatch this forthwith, or face an eternity of litigation.

Yours threateningly,

C. Walpurgis Murray.'

•

A note from his agent in 1980 informed Chic that Bill Forsyth wanted him for two days' filming on *Gregory's Girl* instead of one – for the same money.

'Tell him I'll do half a day for double the money,' he scribbled back. 'PS. If he doesn't agree to that, ask him if he's in full possession of himself.'

•

A bill from the Eccentric Club in London (of which Chic was naturally enough a member) elicited the question, 'Do I get an eccentric discount? And if not, why not?'

•

A missive to Radio Rentals in 1983: 'Enclosed cheque for £2 for tape provided. Do you have such a thing as a video recorder that records programmes you don't want to see and plays them back when you're out?'

•

A postcard to Maidie in 1979: 'Maidie! Trousers are down, hemlines are up, so sell my Burton's shares. And I've just heard that diets are out, so buy United Biscuits. And put five bob each way on Nag's Head in the 2.30 at Newmarket.

Your devoted husband.'

•

Another postcard to Maidie, in 1982: 'I'd walk the burning desert for the touch of your hand. I'd climb the highest mountain for a kind look. I'd swim the deepest river for your gentle touch.

Chic.

PS. I'll be over to see you on Sunday if it doesn't rain.'

•

A letter to Woolworths:

'Dear Sirs,

It has come to my attention that you no longer stock pen nibs. This is nothing short of an outrage. For years you have been peddling pens without nibs, encouraging the gullible public – such as my own good self – to purchase with confidence, in the full and certain knowledge that a limitless supply of nibs would forever be on tap. (Nibs on tap; wouldn't taps on nibs have been better? It might have helped the flow of ink. Just a thought.)

But I digress. Just remember that you can herd pigs into a pen, but a pencil must be led. Suffice to say that if this matter is not rectified before the next full moon you'd better get the garlic out; it'll be a case of "Fangs for the Memory".

Yours graphically, C. Murray Ponderthwaite (deceased)

PS. And the same to you with nibs on.'

•

A letter to John Menzies:

'Dear Sirs,

I wish to report the manager of your Inverkip branch for rudeness over and above the call of duty. The other day he refused to accept my cheque for 12p for a copy of the *Daily Record*. Even when I offered to top this up with a second purchase, that of a 10p packet of rubber hands, he again turned down my preferred method of payment. (Before you ask why I wanted the rubber bands, this is nothing whatever to do with you. In the immortal words of Sir John Barbirolli, "How I conduct my affairs is my own affair".)

Kindly reprimand this reprobate without delay, or the next time I'm within the precincts of Inverkip I will take it upon myself to unload the collection of farthings I have saved for years. Have you ever wondered how many it would take to purchase a copy of the *Encyclopaedia Britannica*? Would you *really* like to find out?

I remain, in the words of our family motto, "Despondent, but not Despairing".

Yours,
Corstorphine Wullie.'

7

THE TERROR OF THE SURGERY

I'm living with my aunt here. Well, she's not really my aunt, I think we've all got them, aunties who are not really aunties. In this case I know it's not my auntie. It's my *uncle* – he just likes to be *called* auntie! He said to me, 'If you're passing the butcher, get a sheep's head, I'll make us some broth.'

I said, 'If I'm passing the butcher, I'll need to go into the butcher.'

'Yes,' he agreed.

'I hope you don't think I'm being too crypto-cratic,' I told him.

'Oh, no,' he said, 'it's just your ways.'

So I was making my way to the butcher's when I felt this sharp pain. I thought, 'Oh, ho!' Wait a minute, was it 'Oh, ho!?' No it wasn't – or was it? Now I've forgotten. This *would* happen. *Was* it 'Oh, ho?' Anyway. So I changed my mind and went to the doctor's instead. I'm very decisive that way. I thought, 'That's it, no butcher's, doctor's instead.'

I made my way into the waiting room. I didn't go into the surgery – you've got to know the doctor fairly well before you can force your way into the surgery. No, I just made my way into the waiting room and sat down. There was a bench, otherwise I would never have attempted it. It also let the rest of the patients there see that I could do it. At least I assumed they were patients. I didn't say, 'Are you a patient?' I'm not a curious person. So I just sat there. And they were looking at me the way I'm looking at you, and we were all wondering what was wrong with each other. After some time the door of the waiting room opened, and I looked – just to give myself something to do. I've seen a door opening before, there was *no novelty* in it!

This fellow came in, a stranger to me. And though there was ample room in the waiting room he chose to sit beside me. He was in very close proximity and I thought I felt a nudge. I wasn't too sure. Then he started speaking to me about this and that, about which I know very little. He said, 'What do you think of this?'

I said, 'Oh, I don't think much of that!' I thought, 'If he comes out with a bag of toffees, *I'm off!*'

So just as I'm contemplating this the door of the surgery opened and the doctor made his entrance. Oh, it was just a small fanfare. I didn't know it was the doctor at first, but 'this and that', he knew it was the doctor. 'Oh, it's the doctor!' he said, and he nodded and the doctor nodded back. I thought, the next time I'm in here, I'll get in quick and say 'It's the doctor!' and he'll nod to me.

The doctor was wearing a kilt – probably a Scottish doctor, though you're never too sure nowadays. Very short, I thought. So short you didn't notice it immediately. He came swinging gaily into the waiting room and he looked at us all – which he's got every right to do, it's his waiting room, he can do what he likes. Then he took a little run and he stood on his hands and said, 'How's that for a shuttlecock?' A few applauded, probably the panel patients – the regulars. Or maybe they were panel beaters, I don't honestly know *what* they were. Then he got back on his feet, which I thought was bound to happen – he couldn't stay up there for long, there must be a limited amount of time you can spend on your Germans. He said, 'Who's next?' And the *rush* for that door, I've never seen anything like it in my life. I don't know *how* I managed to get in first!

The doctor looked pleased, I knew he was pleased the way he shut the door. He said, 'You're new.'

I said, 'I'm hardly unwrapped.'

He said, 'I like someone who's new. What is it?'

I said, 'I don't know what it is.'

His expression changed. He said, 'Oh, I don't like this. I *detest* when patients come in and they don't know what it is. Makes it so difficult for me. It means I've got to go into that little room at the end there and look up the medical dictionary. It could be anything you've got and my eyes aren't up to all that reading. What do *you* think it is?'

I said, 'I don't know what it is.'

He said, 'Well, there must be something. Talk to me.'

I said, 'Well, I get a pain about six inches above my head.'

'Oh,' he said, 'I could cure that. I'll give you something to take half an hour before you wake up! How long have you had this?'

I said, 'I've had it before.'

'So it's recurring?'

'You could say that.'

'I've just said it and I've no intention of saying

41

it again. Been going on for a few years, then?'

I said, 'Yes.'

'Have you got a war record?' he asked. I replied that I had. He said, 'What is it?'

'It's Vera Lynn singing "The White Cliffs of Dover",' I told him.

He said, 'I like that. I'm beginning to take a personal interest in you. You'd better strip off. *Strip!*'

'Don't you think you should take me out a couple of times first?' I asked.

'Take them off,' he insisted, utterly undeterred.

'Where do I put them?' I asked.

He said, 'Put them on top of mine! Now then, I want to see you walk. We doctors can tell a lot from a walk. That's it, walk! Mmm, uh huh, mmm, uh huh, you turn nicely.' (I had to turn, I was up against a wall. I just did it on my own initiative.) He said, 'Excellent! That's a *great* walk you've got. That's the best walk we've had in the surgery. I wish my partner were here. He's always out on these occasions. *Brilliant* walk. Have you been practising?'

I said, 'No, I haven't.' (I do a nice walk, I know that.)

'Let me see you do it again,' he asked. He was really pleased, I could see that. He patted me and said, 'Well done.' He missed me the second time, I shortened my step. He said, 'I hope you don't mind.'

'Oh,' I said, 'Feel free.'

'There's only one thing,' he said, 'you're swaying a little. Mind you, it's not unseemly. Oh, no, I quite like it. But have you been drinking any of that pansy wine?'

I said, 'No, I have not.'

'Is it something you ate then?' he persisted.

'Well, perhaps, doctor,' I replied. 'Yesterday I had a little roast peasant.'

'Oh,' he said, 'I'm a doctor of medicine, I'm not a teacher of elocution, but it's not a peasant, it's normally a phartridge.'

He said, 'You'd better bend over.' I did that. He said, 'You're blushing.' I don't know how he knew that. He said, 'You're covered with tattoos, too. Hey, that's an interesting one, that fox disappearing up . . . I must have a look at that some time.'

In bending over I had positioned myself *badly*, for suddenly the door burst open. I'd never thought of a door knob like that before. I had a look between my legs just to see who it was, and it was a huge fellow built like a rugby threequarter who was obviously the doctor's partner. I straightened up quickly and said, 'Doctor!' with a little gesture of surprise.

He said, 'Don't call me doctor, don't be so formal, I feel as if I know you. From now on it's first names. Call me Lance.'

I said, 'Well, Lance, could you write me out a prescription?'

So I left the surgery – their entreaties notwithstanding – and made my way into the nearest chemist. 'Is the apothecary in?' I asked.

'No,' this fellow behind the counter replied.

'How about the pharmacist?' I said.

'No, there's just me, the chemist,' he told me.

Just then a woman came in with a rush. She put the rush on a chair. Nice little thing it was.

'What is it?' I asked her. She said it was her ulcer.

I said, 'There's no need to call me sir!'

The chemist said, 'What is it with you?'

I said, 'I've got a message from the front.'

'Oh,' he said, 'I haven't had one of those for years. How did you manage it? Were you followed?'

'No,' I said.

'Good,' he said. 'Oh, you're due some pills. Will I put them in a box?'

'Well,' I told him, 'it'll save me rolling them all the way home!'

8

GIDDY LIMITS – I

The Irish duck-hunting team returned despondently to their clubhouse without a single bird. 'Maybe we're not throwing our dogs high enough,' one of them suggested.

•

I'm all in favour of the new rules at football games, especially the one about always empty-ing a bottle of beer before throwing it at the referee.

•

Friends, my grandfather was a politician, my father was a politician, I'm a politician – and my son's not going to work either!

•

There were two elderly ladies, both of them old friends, travelling together on a plane. 'Wouldn't it be terrible if we fell out?' said one.
    'Och, we've been friends for too long for that to happen,' the other replied.

•

Mrs Brown in our close keeps her age very quiet.

But I heard that her birthday cake collapsed under the weight of the candles.

●

I passed our vicar the other day. 'Hello, Father,' I greeted him. 'Still on a one-day week?'

●

An old girlfrield of mine once pointed out that I'd never remarked on her glass eye. I told her it must be the left eye, the only one with a spark of humanity in it.

●

My pal Jimmy has a terrible inferiority complex. When the rest of the rugby team go into a scrum he thinks they're talking about him. In his will he's requested that his hearse follows the other cars at his funeral.

●

'I can't decide where to go,' the flustered lady said to her travel agent.

'Look,' he said, 'I'll leave you with this globe of the world for ten minutes. It should help you make up your mind.' When he came back he looked at her hopefully.

'Well?'

'Have you got another globe?' she asked.

●

I went up to this fellow in Paris, hoping to impress him. *'Vive la France, fermez la porte, Maurice Chevalier,'* I said. He was quite surprised. He was a Dutchman.

●

My boss is so narrow-minded that when he has an idea it comes out folded.

●

We have a wonderful magician who works in the BBC. He can squeeze ninety-two double whiskies from an ordinary bottle. He's known as a barman.

●

I met this cowboy with a brown paper hat, paper waistcoat and paper trousers. He told me he was wanted for rustling.

●

I first met my wife in the Tunnel of Love. She was digging it.

●

My sister fell asleep on her water bed. The house went on fire and she was poached to death.

●

Have you heard the great new tune that's just got into the Irish Top Twenty at number 36?

●

We live in a very nervous neighbourhood. Even my dustbin's got ulcers.

●

Algernon lives by his wits. That accounts for the half-starved look on his face.

●

When politicians tell us they want to serve the public, we farmers know what they mean. Like the bull serves the cow!

•

Why is it that some girls always get salary increases after every office party?

•

I was stopped by the police on the M1 and told it was a spot check. I admitted to two pimples and a boil.

•

My uncle's a born loser. If he cornered the mistletoe market they'd cancel Christmas.

•

My wife gave me a present of an atomic-powered watch that doesn't lose a single second in 10,000 years. It came with a three-month guarantee.

9

LOOPY LIMERICKS

There was a young lady named Harris,
Whom nothing could seem to embarrass,
Till the bath salts she shook,
In a bath that she took,
Turned out to be plaster of Paris.

•

Bruised by the masseur's final whack,
I lay without a sound,
Coming to, I hit him back,
Now he's in the cold, cold ground.

•

A baritone famed of Havana,
Slipped arse over tit on a 'nana,
He was sick for a year,
Then resumed his career,
As a promising mezzo-soprano.

•

The boy stood on the burning deck,
Would he wash his dirty neck?
Would he heck!

•

There once was a lady named Lily,
Who walked up and down Piccadilly,
Said she, 'Ain't it funny,
It's not for the money,
But if I don't take it, it's silly!'

•

Georgie, porgie, puddin' and pie,
Kissed the girls and made them cry,
When the boys came out to play,
He kissed them too. He's funny that way.

•

A wartime young lady of fashion,
Much noted for wit and for passion,
Is known to have said,
As she jumped into bed,
'Here's one thing those bastards can't ration!'

•

The boy stood on the burning deck,
Eating a tenpenny Walls,
A bit ran down his trouser leg,
And paralyzed his balls.

•

When I awoke this morning,
When all sweet things are born,
A robin perched upon my sill,
To greet the coming morn.
Its song was sweet and beautiful,
It filled my heartfelt need,
I gently closed the window,
And crushed its bleedin' heid.

•

There was a young lady of Dee,
Went to bed with each man she could see,
When it came to a test,
She wished to be best.
And practice makes perfect, you see.

10

TALL-ISH TALES

On the way to the studio today I got off the main road. I didn't mean to, it occurred because I wasn't looking where I was going. I crossed a farm track and I ran over a cockerel. Pardon? A *cockerel*. I'll say it again – I ran over this rooster, or cockerel, or whatever it was. It was just a mass of feathers. I said, 'Oh goodness gracious me!' or something else appertaining which I felt appropriate to the occasion. I got out the car and followed the farm track all the way up to the farm. Eventually I came across this lady. I said, 'Look, I've just run over a cockerel. Well, *I* didn't actually – it was the *car* I was driving that ran over it.'

'Oh,' said she. 'You ran over Hector?'

I thought, 'Oh, God, he was one of the family!' So I said, 'Well look, I'm extremely sorry – and as a matter of fact I'd like to replace it.'

'Oh,' she said. 'Please yourself. The hens are round the back!'

•

An Indian stood on a street corner and every time a pretty woman came by he raised his left hand and said 'When'. Eventually, as a beautiful blonde passed, he raised his hand once more and repeated, 'When'.

'But I thought all Indians said "How",' said the blonde.

'Me know how,' the brave replied. 'Me want to know when!'

•

I remember one New Year at Murray McEwan's house – or was it Ewan McMurray's? Anyway, it was a house, because I remember going through the door. In fact, mine was his first foot through the door – my right foot, right through the cat flap! Which was a bit unfortunate for the cat, who happened to be coming out at the time.

Blackie I think it was called – but I didn't have any time for introductions, for at the very moment my foot went through the flap, Ewan McMurray, or Murray McEwan, or whatever he was called, decided to open the door. Well, I've had my leg pulled before, but never when it was stuck in a cat flap.

So down I went – flat on my back on the doorstep. It was just as well I had my bottle in my hand. Ewan or Murray looked at me and said, 'Oh, hello, Thomas, drunk already?' I thought this was a bit uncalled for, because my name's not Thomas for a start. I didn't say anything, though. I couldn't – because the cat was sitting on my face. A friendly beast.

Then the host looked down at me and said, 'My, that's a big lump of coal you've brought. Come on in.' So I went in – and threw the cat on the fire.

And then I treated the crowd to a performance on my harmonica. In the wave of silence that followed, this woman, who shall remain nameless – largely because I can't remember her name –

said, 'Without doubt, that is the finest performance of Gilbert and Sullivan that I have ever—'

I think she was about to say 'heard', when she passed out. Overcome by emotion, no doubt.

●

A bachelor friend of mine visited the Ideal Home Exhibition at Olympia and bought an ironing table. He wanted one that could be compressed into a small space and extend whenever he wanted to do – well, whatever he intended to do with it, I suppose.

When he got to Euston he found that the sleeping compartment he had booked had been given up. There was an air strike on, the train was packed, and he found himself having to share a four-berth compartment. He made his way up to one of the top berths and tucked his ironing table neatly away at the back. Idly glancing at the bunk opposite, he noticed a female looking at him. 'What's happened here?' he asked. 'I thought this was . . .'

'Oh, it's been dreadful,' she told him. 'I had a first-class sleeper all to myself, but the way things are I'm just so pleased to get in here.'

So he didn't waste a minute. Ignoring the two fellows in the berths below them, he said, 'Why don't you slip over to my bunk and share a cigarette with me?'

'Oh,' she said, 'I don't even know you.'

'Don't let that worry you,' he said. 'I have a feeling we'll soon put that right.'

'Well, even if I did want to come over to your bunk,' she said, 'I still couldn't manage it. I'd disturb the occupants of the bunks below and I don't even know where that silly little ladder's got to.'

'You don't need that silly little ladder,' my friend assured her.

'I don't?' she asked.

'No,' he replied. 'I've got a little something here that could stretch over to your bunk and you could walk across on it.'

'Just then an incredulous voice from below said, 'I don't *believe* it!' Then, a few seconds later, 'And anyway, how's she going to get back?'

•

Lady: Oh, Jeeves, you know that my boyfriend Donald returns from five years in India today?

Butler: Yes, miss. No doubt he'll be very pleased to see you after all that time.

Lady: Precisely. So ring me the moment he appears, there's a good fellow.

One hour later, the boyfriend's back

Donald: How are you, Jeeves? I say, is Mabel about? I daresay she'll be rather anxious to see me.

Butler: As a matter of fact, sir, she told me to ring her the moment you arrived.

Donald: Jolly good! But I say, Jeeves, don't ring just yet. I've been away a long time and I'm just a teensy bit nervous about what she might ask me.

Butler: Quite, sir. Well, I'd imagine the question uppermost in her mind is if you've been with any other ladies while you were away, sir.

Donald: Good heavens, Jeeves, that'll be an awkward one.

Butler: Oh, I see, sir. Well sir, if you're a little bit dubious, might I suggest that if you're going to tell a lie, you make it appear like the truth. Don't hesitate, be forthright, come right out with it.

Donald: You seem to know all about it, Jeeves.

Butler: Well, I'm married sir. Now the first question she'll ask is, 'Have you been with any other girl?' You must be very dramatic and positive about it and answer, 'Darling, of course not, how could I?'

Donald: I see. 'Darling, of course not, how could I? Darling, of course not, how could I? Darling, of course not, how could I.'

Butler: You've got it sir. Now I'll ring for m'lady.

Enter Mabel, a vision of loveliness in a simple polka-dot, ankle-length chemise

Donald (*as butler discreetly withdraws*): Mabel!

Mabel: Donald! My own!

They embrace, then

Mabel: Tell me, Donald, while you've been away, have you been faithful to me?

Donald: Darling, of course not, how could I?

•

Two pals had been meeting for years for a week-end drink in a pub just outside their village. Tam was a hunchback; Jock had a club foot.

One night, after they were well oiled, Tam said, 'The hell with it. Ah'm no for gawn the long way hame the night. Ah'm cuttin' through the grave-yard.'

'You're a braver man than me,' said Jock. 'But here – let me gie ye a leg up o'er the wa'.'

As Tam was making his way through the graveyard, a hooded, mist-enshrouded apparition appeared and surveyed him. 'Here, you,' said the apparition, 'what's that on your back?'

'It's just ma hump,' said Tam.

At this the apparition approached him and effortlessly lifted it off.

The following weekend the two friends met as usual in the pub. Jock was amazed to see Tam's hump gone and was treated to the whole story. 'Here,' he said, 'maybe if Ah walked through the graveyard the ghostie would get rid of ma club foot. It's worth a shot.'

'Go on yoursel',' said Tam, 'once was enough for me. But Ah'll gie ye a leg up o'er the wa' same as ye did for me.'

Sure enough, as Jock was making his way through the graveyard, the apparition again materialized. 'Here, you,' it said, 'what's that on your back?'

'Nothin',' said Jock.

'Well, here's a hump for you, then.'

11

WHAT IS A SCOT?

What is a Scot? I keep getting asked that. He's a man who keeps the Sabbath, that's for sure – and everything else he can lay his hands on.

Are all these stories about Aberdonians true? Well, you can judge for yourself. My dad was an Aberdonian and a more generous man you couldn't wish to meet. I have a gold watch that belonged to him. He sold it to me on his death bed. I wrote him a cheque for it – post-dated, of course.

Please don't think that all Aberdonians are money-grabbers, though. That would be an erroneous impression. It's simply that the mint makes it first, and they feel they've got to make it last.

As to the myth of Scots in general being mean, are we forgetting so soon that it was a Scot who offered £50,000 to the first man to swim the Atlantic in gumboots? This same worthy claimed that his grandfather was the most successful business man of all times. When a rival in London asked for the secret of his success, he told him it was all a matter of 'brain food'. He then offered his rival a course of this food, at two guineas a time.

Each week thereafter he sent him a pair of

kippers that cost him two shillings. Six months and 48 guineas later, he received a letter stating:

'Dear Mr Carnegie,
I have had the feeling for some months that 2 guineas is rather a high price to pay for a pair of kippers. I am now almost convinced that the charge is too heavy. Please advise.'

Carnegie was fully equal to these aspersions and wired back: 'Continue course. It is at last beginning to show results.'

Scotland has so many other things to recommend it. We gave the world golf, for example. St Andrews is the home of golf, but I'm sure St Andrew himself never played it. If he had, he'd never have been made a saint.

I don't like to boast, but I'm an excellent golfer myself. Straight down the middle, that's me. It will give you an idea of how good I am when I tell you that last week I lost my first ball in ten years. The string broke.

I was taught golf by an old Scottish professional, a real purist. I'll never forget the first morning I went out on the tee. He gave me a seven iron and I was so nervous I could hardly hold the club. He placed the ball on the tee, and taking my courage in both hands, I swung at the ball. To my amazement and delight it flew through the air right on to the green and landed in the cup. I stood there awaiting congratulations. 'No, no, laddie, that'll no do at a' at a',' he said, 'you're using the wrong grip!'

It's true that the Scots are devoted to their golf. A friend of mine was once about to try a particularly difficult putt on a green near the main road. A funeral passed by just at that moment, and he stopped and took his bunnet off. 'I didn't think you were as respectful as all that,' I said.

'It was the least I could do,' he replied. 'She was a good wife to me.'

The other thing we always associate with the Scots is drinking, mainly whisky, which is our national drink. There are only two rules for imbibing this magic liquid. First, never take whisky without water. Second, never take water without whisky.

The Scot is very proud of being able to hold his drink. I remember being out with a friend of mine one night and having had a great time. The next morning I met him. 'You had a real skinful last night,' I observed. 'Did you manage to make it home all right?'

'I was getting home fine,' he replied. 'My mistake was in stopping to rest in the gutter for a minute. That's when this big stupid policeman stood on my fingers.'

I heard recently of a Scot on holiday in London who had been out on a bender. On his way home he was set upon by a bunch of muggers. A born fighter, the Scot put up a very stubborn resistance before finally being overpowered after a long and bloody fight.

The leader of the gang expected a large bounty after such an epic struggle and was disappointed, when turning his pockets out to find that the Scot had but a single ten pence piece on him. 'Imagine,' he said to the rest of the gang, 'only ten pence after that monumental struggle.' One of his mates chimed in. 'Maybe we're in luck. Imagine the fight he'd have put up for twenty pence!'

12

FILM FUN

Chic was an avid film fan, dating back to Flash Gordon serials, Bill Boyd Westerns, Boston Blackie gangsters, W.C. Fields and Mae West comedies, the Bowery Boys series – you name it, Chic was there, absorbing it all. So perhaps it was only natural that in the notes he left on his school jotters were many comical sketches for movies *he* intended to make!

Andrew Yule

CHIC MURRAY
(in association with PIPING HOT CURRY
IN A HELLUVA HURRY PRODUCTIONS)

presents

LOITERING WITHIN TENT

An Epic Tale Of The Big Top!

(freely adapted from
THE END OF THE TRAIL
by KIRT AINS)

starring

Charles	Tom	Ellie
HAWTRE JR	**FOOLERY**	**VATE**
as	as	as
Tough	Rollicking	Battling
ROCK	**COCO**	**BELLA**
O'IRON	**LOCO**	**HUSTON**
The World's	The World's	The World's
Strongest	Unfunniest	Lowest
Man	Clown!	High-Wire Artiste!

with

Liz	Bob	John E.	Effy	Marie	Sean E.	Mark
ARD	**AJOB**	**BEATTIE**	**GEE**	**NATE**	**RIVER**	**TYME**

and THE MASSED PIPES AND DRUMS OF THE LOGAN FAMILY!!

Music	*Production Design*	*Script*	*Producer*	*Director*
Nick L.	Lynn	Penny	Dirk	Annie
ODEON	**OLEUM**	**TENT**	**HEAD**	**MATE**

CHIC MURRAY
(for LIVING ON BORROWED TIME PRODUCTIONS)

presents

BUNGLE IN THE JUNGLE

Revealed! The Monkey Business They Tried To Cover Up!

(blazingly adapted from the novel, DOWN THE TUBES by LESTER SQUARE AND EARL SKORT)

starring

MARCEL	BELLA
O'PHANE	DONNA
as	as
SINGING JACK	BOUNCING BETTY
BLOOMSBURY	BLOOMSBURY

with

Fred	Greg	Sam	Nick R	Harrison	June
RICK	ARIOUS	PELL	LASTIC	TWEED	IPER

Anna	Lou Dick
CONDA	RUSS

Monster Make Up	*Catering*	*Script*	*Producer*	*Director*
Frank N.	Gordon	Ann O.	Blake	Algernon
STEIN	BLUE	DYNE	HOUSE	ENTITY

CHIC MURRAY

(in association with READY, READY,
TEDDY TO ROCK & ROLL
PRODUCTIONS)

presents

A FARE TO REMEMBER

Exposed Scandal on The Buses!

(Adapted stop by stop from
THYME TABLES,
A Guide to Herbal Gardens
by ALBIE TROSS)

starring

Brad	Luke	Nana	Val E.
FORD	ALIKE	SKIN	DATE
as	as	as	as
Cal	Bill	Ann	Al A.
ABOOSE	ABONG	TWERP	CARTE

—Ringing Up Fares Was Only A Cover-Up For Their Baby-Sitting Racket!—

with

Mel	Jock	Axminster
IFFLUOUS	ULAR	ELDERBERRY

Polly	Ann U.	Sid
ANNA	ALL	KNEE

Catering	*Script*	*Producer*	*Co-Producer*	*Location*	*Director*
Bo	Lee Bert	Brian	Polly	Beryl	Ray
JOLAY	EINE	O'BRITTEN	ANNA	INN	VERRE

CHIC MURRAY

(in association with MO MENTOUS, JUSTIN TYME & DES TINNY PRODUCTIONS)

presents

BETWEEN THE SHEETS

A Searing Drama Of Life, Love And Deadlines!

(strenuously adapted from the novel, HOLD THE FRONT PAGE! by IVOR BIGGUN)

starring

Bill O' THEBELT	Sam ANTHA
as	as
'UNLUCKY' LUKE MUCKRAKER 'SMALL ADS' ACE!	'MUDDLED' ESTHER O'FLAHERTY III RACING TIPSTRESS EXTRAORDINAIRE!

with

Kate ASTROPHE	Dan AIR	Pat RICK	Amy Lee ORATE	Jon QUIL	Jim E. LOGAN

Mel
BOURNE

Script	*UK Locations*	*Italian Locations*	*Security*
Cliff HANGER	M. BANKMENT	Don ATELLO	Chuck OUT

Producer	*Director*
Leo NINE	Jay WALKER

CHIC MURRAY
(in association with THREE SHEETS TO
THE WIND PRODUCTIONS)

presents

THE
LEGEND
OF MARK
O. POLO

His Life! His Loves!! His Flatulence!!!

(vaguely adapted from the novel,
CHINESE TINKLES
by XYLO PHONE)

starring

Albie	Donna
TROSS	**KEBAB**
as	as
WILD, UNTAMED POLO	SADIE SOUVLAKI
The TOO-GOOD-TO-HURRY	the TOO-HOT-TO-HANDLE
VENETIAN!	TURKISH TAKEAWAY!
(HIS MOTTO – 'WHERE'RE YOU BE,	(HER MOTTO – 'DON'T
LET THE WIND GO FREE!')	CALL UPON US, WE'LL CALL
	UPON YOU!')

with

O.B.	Blair	Ruth	Pru	Herb
QUIET	**GOWRIE**	**LESS**	**DENTIAL**	**GARDEN**

Mick E.
MOUSE

Catering	*Music*	*Accountant*	*Script*	*Producer*	*Director*
Hal E.	Dan	Val	O. Kent	Peter	Anton
BUT	**DERUNDUN**	**EWE**	**ROAD**	**SHAM**	**IONI**

CHIC MURRAY

(in association with SPARE PRICK AT A
WEDDING PRODUCIONS)

presents

ONE NIGHT IN PHILADELPHIA

In Or Out Of Love – It Seemed Like
A Fortnight!

(outrageously adapted from SEVEN
MINUTES BEFORE THE MAST,
The Story Of The World's Shortest Naval
Apprenticeship –
Told By
The World's Shortest Naval
Apprentice, Jack 'Tiny Bubbles' O'Tar)

Starring

Mal	Norma
EVOLENT	LIZE
as	as
DEVIL-MAY-CARE	BATTLING
RORY 'LOOSELIPS'	BESSIE
McSLUDGE	BALONEY

with

Don	B.	Hazel	Clark	Ruth	Steve E.
ATION	RATE	NUT	ENWELL	LESS	DORE

Production Design	*Cameraman*	*Catering*	*Script*	*Director*
Con	Biff	Cole	O.	Pat
ARTIST	OCAL	SLAW	PEN	ERNITY

Producer
Ho
KUM

CHIC MURRAY

(in association with HONG KONG
PHOOEY UNLIMITED PRODUCTIONS)

presents

THE
LEGEND OF
HARRY KIRI

His Antics Covered Three Continents!

(arrestingly adapted from the novel,
REACH FOR YOUR WALLET
by HANS UPP)

starring

Rick SHAW as BIG TIGHTWAD McGURK – SCOURGE OF THE KUNG FU ACADEMY!	Care Fu LEE as MAD SEAMUS McSHAUGHNESSY – THE WAN-CHAU WIMP!	Pola ROID as SERENDIPITY O'TOOLE – EVERY NEW MAN WAS ANOTHER NOTCH ON HER KIMONO!

with

Percival POLICELLO	Nat WEST	Ellie PHANT	Cloris BLEACHMAN	Des PERATE

Gerry
ATRIC

Mo
DERATE

Choreography Morrie DANCE	*Costume Design* E. Paul ETTE	*Catering* Cal ORY	*Script* Alma NACK

Producer
Wun Hung
LO

Director
Simon
EYES

CHIC MURRAY

(in association with HANGING BY A
THREAD PRODUCTIONS)

presents

THE BIG
YARN
RIPOFF

Torn From Tomorrow's Headlines!

(loosely adapted from the novel,
CONSTIPATION BLUES
by I.B. BUNGFU
and the sequel, FREED AT LAST
by GREGOR E. SPOWDER)

starring

Terry	Polly
LENE	ESTER
as	as
RICK O'SHEA	SHIMMERING FATIMA
	O'CALLAGHAN

with

| Belle | Viv | Hugh | Mae | Monte |
| GRADE | ACIOUS | JARSE | NIAK | ZUMA |

| Rick E. | Lorne A. |
| FULTON | DOONE |

Musical Score	*Sound Recordist*	*Sword-Fencing Adviser*
Mel	Mike	Ray
O'TRON	ROFONE	PIERRE

Script	*Producer*	*Director*
Ben	Herbie	O. Hugh
ZEDRINE	VORE	CARES

CHIC MURRAY

(in association with MGM, COLUMBIA, UNIVERSAL,
& Anyone Else Mug Enough To Throw In
A Bob Or Two)

presents

JESSIE

Married – But Misses His Mammy!
What Is He To Do?!

(liberally adapted from the novel,
PLACE YOUR BETS
by AVA GAMBLE)

starring

Nick	Anne	Marti	Vera
ERAGUA	ACHRONISM	NETTE	CITY
as	as	as	as
'WORRIED'	'SULTRY'	BIG	AUNT
JESS KIDDIN	LIL KIDDIN	MAMMY	SALLY
		MIA	FORTH

with

Kirby	Randy	Alex	Lou	Sam U.	Kate A.
GRIP	B'ASTARD	ANDRIA	PINE	RAI	PULT

Catering	*Stuntman*	*Script*	*Producer*	*Director*
Artie	Dexter	Emma	Rip	Siegried
CHOKE	ITTY	NATE	TABITS	TWITWORTHY

13

MEDICAL MADNESS

I had a bad cough and went to the doctor. He gave me some medicine. Now I've got a good cough.

•

'Doctor, if I give up drink, tobacco and sex, will I live longer?'
   'No, it'll only seem longer.'

•

'I'd like a vasectomy, doctor.'
   'With a face like yours, you don't need to bother.'

•

'Doctor, I can't sleep, I'm so scared.'
   'Have you tried counting sheep?'
   'I can't, I'm afraid of them.'

•

'I've just had all my teeth out.'
   'How do you feel?'
   'Never again!'

•

'Doctor, I'm losing my hair.'

'Why don't you have a transplant?'
'Och, I'd look silly with a kidney up there.'

•

'Medical science has made tremendous strides.'
'Thank goodness, I was glad to see the back of those leeches.'

•

'Doctor, I'm losing blood.'
'No, you're not, it's just seeping into your coat.'

•

'You shouldn't drink so much.'
'But, doctor, think of the exercise I get when I hiccup.'

•

There's a new slimming course just out where the doctor removes all your bones. Not only do you weigh less, but you look so much more relaxed.

•

The doctor rushed through the ward to find out what all the noise was about. He was just in time to see a nurse leaving a screaming patient, a bowl of steaming hot water in her hand.

'Oh, *no*, nurse,' he said. 'I told you to *prick* his *boil*.'

14

CHIC'S RANDOM THOUGHTS

I still have lots of friends in showbusiness. Johnny Beattie and I have so much in common. We're both incredibly common. And did you know that when Des O'Connor first began in show business his name on the bill was so small everyone thought he was the printer? Roger Moore? They call him The Man With The Golden Overdraft. Googie Withers? Don't worry – everyone's does in the cold weather. Paul Daniels? Now there's a name to conjure with! By the way, I hear that Jimmy Clitheroe's starring in a revival of *Tiddler on the Roof*. I wouldn't call Sean Connery ostentatious. But he's got four Rolls-Royces – one for each direction.

Another pal's only claim to fame is having fallen off a camel as a child. I won't mention his name, Billy Connolly's had enough bad publicity recently.

A friend of mine named Alex is cricket mad. It's all he dreams about. 'Don't you ever dream about women?' I asked him. 'What?' he said. 'And miss my chance to bat?' All *my* dreams are in black and white nowadays. Mostly repeats, as well. I tried to cheer myself up the other day by going to a gay 90s party. It didn't work. The men were all gay and the women were all 90.

I remember discussing with Bill Forsyth the prospects for *Gregory's Girl* before it was released. He thought it would go down well. 'Yes, yes,' I told him, 'but how will it play at the Plaza, Inverkip?!'

I was sat in my bath the other day playing 'Amazing Grace' on my bagpipe. A plumber walked in and explained that a blockage had been reported. 'Do you think you could change your tune?' he asked, 'and make it "Please Release Me" on the drainpipe?' An impertinent bounder.

I went to a medium the other day and she told me I'd be visited by three spirits – Nancy Whisky, Alec Guinness and Marlon Brandy.

I once knew a man who was so mean he pinched walking sticks from a Darby and Joan club. He died while drinking a glass of beer. Luckily it wasn't wasted, his wife finished it for him. If she hadn't, his spirit would still be roaming the earth.

My new girlfriend's a stoater, but cheeky with it. When I asked her where she'd been all my life, she said, 'Well, for the first 35 years I wasn't born.' But you've got to give as good as you get. When she asked me later where I'd learned to kiss like I did, I said, 'Playing "The Flight Of The Bumble Bee" on a sweet potato. Care for another chorus?'

I was staying in a hotel in London last week and when I got back at night noticed a sign outside, 'Dogs must be carried'. Isn't that daft? Where are you supposed to lay your hands on a dog at midnight?

The boy living next door to us had to get married recently. He's only eleven, but he'd won a honeymoon trip to Bermuda!

I did up the house a few weeks ago. My big mistake was using self-raising flour to stick the wallpaper. Now every time I put the fire on, the walls come up like sponge cake.

One day I was walking along Sauchiehall Street, minding my own business, when I felt a tap on my shoulder. I thought, 'Funny place for a tap.'

At the pictures last night this man approached me. 'That's my seat,' he said.

'I got here first,' I informed him, 'and I'm not budging.'

'Please yourself,' he said. 'I just hope you can play the organ.'

I went into Glasgow by bus the other day and there were two people talking behind me. This man said he'd been in his girlfriend's house watching the latest episode of an exciting serial on television when the set had flickered and conked out. His companion in the bus looked at him and asked what he had done about it. I think the answer was going to be hilariously funny, but that's when I had to get off the bus.

15

Q & A

Life, I've found, is full of questions. Questions, questions, questions. And it's not always easy to find the answers! On the other hand, I knew a girl once who knew all the answers – but didn't know what the questions were! So here are a few questions, complete, for your convenience, with the answers.

Chic

Wee boy: Can you change this toilet roll for five Senior Service?

Shopkeeper: Why?

Wee boy: Our visitors didn't turn up.

•

Archie: I want a blind dog for my mother-in-law.

Pet shopkeeper: You mean a guide dog?

Archie: No, I mean a blind dog. If he saw her, it would go for her throat.

•

Wee boy:	Grandpa, will you kick this bucket?
Grandpa:	Why?
Wee boy:	Because Mum told Dad last night I'd get a new bike when you did.

•

| Douglas: | Am I really the only man in your life? |
| Flo: | Of course you are, darling. Gosh, I don't know why you men always ask the same stupid question! |

•

| Jock: | Can I make love to you? I want to do it so badly. |
| Maisie: | You always did, darling. |

•

| Ernest: | Hold me tight. |
| Vanessa: | Hold your tight what? |

•

| Husband: | Darling, our love could last till the end of time. |
| Wife: | Aye, fifteen minutes each way, and penalties. |

•

| Maggie: | How could you make love to that woman behind my back? |

Sanny: With great difficulty, I'd imagine.

●

Patient: I'd rather have a baby than visit
               the dentist.

Dentist: Fine, I'll adjust the chair.

●

Wife: Have you got the brochures?

Husband: No, it's just these tight trousers
               I'm wearing.

●

Judge: I'll have to take out a Sabrina.

Attorney: Surely, m'lud, you mean sub-
               poena.

Judge: You take out what you want and
               I'll take out what I want.

●

Ernie: We'll have some champagne
               with the meal. But make sure it's
               the right voltage.

Waiter: Don't you mean vintage, sir?

Ernie: Your prices are so shocking I
               think voltage is more appro-
               priate.

●

Punter: Can anyone with money join this
               game?

Cardsharp:	Yes, if you don't mind being separated from it.

•

Rab:	I just swallowed a cricket ball.
Doctor:	Howzat?
Rab:	Don't you start!

•

Instructor:	Deplane at 3,000 feet and don't pull the ripcord until you're four feet from the ground.
Trainee:	Are you kidding?
Instructor:	Why, what's the matter? Are you scared of jumping a mere four feet?

•

Banker:	Do you have collateral?
Applicant:	No, it's just the way I cross my legs.

•

Algernon:	Do you believe in a Fairy God-mother?
Ignatius:	No, but we've an uncle we're keeping an eye on.

•

Patient:	Doctor, I've got three minutes to live. Can you do anything for me?'

Doctor:	I could boil you an egg.

●

Marie:	Am I the first girl you've ever made love to?'
Tam:	Possibly. Were you behind the aircraft hangar at Glasgow Airport in December, 1959?

●

Policeman:	If you're not drunk, what are you doing down there in the gutter?
Motorist:	I found a parking space and sent the wife home to get the car.

●

Paddy:	I'd like a car wash.
Attendant:	OK, Paddy.
Paddy:	How do you know I'm Irish?
Attendant:	We don't get many motor bikes in here.

●

Wife:	My husband hasn't spent a single penny in the last six months.
Neighbour:	What's he been doing?
Wife:	Six months.

●

Kathleen:	Our Patrick's up before the court for interfering with young girls.

Neighbour:	But surely he's been up before for interfering with young boys?
Kathleen:	Aye, that's right. Sure it's a step in the right direction!

•

Alex:	My wife and I haven't spoken to each other for two years.
Neighbour:	Did you have a row?
Alex:	No, we just can't think of anything to say to each other.

•

Dad:	Our baby swallowed a fountain pen when you were out.
Mum:	What have you done about it?
Dad:	I used a pencil.

•

Dad:	Do you know the *Barber of Seville*?
Son:	Yes.
Dad:	Get your haircut, then.

•

Sid:	I've invented *Crabis Reversus*.
Andy:	What's that?
Sid:	It's a crab that walks backwards instead of sideways.

•

Bedouin:	Tell these screaming women I'll see them later in my tent.
Slave:	They're not screaming.
Bedouin:	They're not in my tent yet.

•

Mo:	Waiter, there's a fly swimming in my soup.
Waiter:	Really? I must have given you too much. It should only be paddling.

•

Mum:	Where do bad boys go when they steal?
Wee boy:	Woolworth's.

•

Fred:	Are you superstitious?
Dan:	No, not at all.
Fred:	Lend me £13, then.

•

Teacher:	Where's Uganda?
Wee boy:	Buried next to my grandma.

•

Paddy:	I want some nails.
Ironmonger:	How long do you want them?
Paddy:	For good.

•

Stu:	I had to take my dog to the vet.
Neighbour:	Why?
Stu:	It bit my mother-in-law.
Neighbour:	Did you have it put down?
Stu:	No, I had its teeth sharpened.

●

Father:	Don't get supercilious with me, son.
Wee boy:	What does that mean?
Father:	I don't know, but it's worth eighteen points at scrabble.

●

Bridie:	Paddy, go down to the corner and get some cockroach powder.
Paddy:	OK, Mam.
Bridie:	And don't tell them what we want it for!

ABOVE, Chic's military pass for the team's visit to entertain the troops in Cyprus – the prelude to Chic and Maidie's bomb scare, as hilariously described in *The Best Way To Walk*. BELOW, one of the notebooks, school jotters and scribbling pads Chic covered with new ideas – the source of much of the material in the current volume, and RIGHT, private studies of Chic, courtesy of The Maidie Murray Collection (i.e. the trunk under her bed).

LEFT, Chic and Maidie at their peak, and
RIGHT, Top of the Bill.

EMPIRE THEATRE
GLASGOW

TOM ARNOLD

Brings You

5 of Scotland's Greatest Headliners

in

"Just Daft"

Opens
DEC.
13th

Stars ... ES HENRY

...HIC
...RAY

AND MAIDIE

...LIANT
...EASON
OR

AUTUMN VAUDEVILLE PRESENTATION

NEXT WEEK

Featuring Our Special Guest Star
Stage, Radio & T.V. Personality

CHIC MURRAY

with MAIDIE

Supported by a Star Company including

NICKY KIDD   SAMMY SHORTT
Betty Melville   Lawrie Adam
Bill Cameron   Neil Owen

George   The Gaiety Dancers   Irene
CORMACK   and   **SHARP**

Programme No. 2.

The Show is Directed by Bill Cameron

When In Glasgow — You Must Visit

The PAVILION Theatre

Currently Presenting

"AUTUMN SHOWTIME"

starring BILLY RUSK
with an all star cast

Presented Twice Nightly

6.25   8.35

ECCENTRIC CLUB
RYDER STREET,
ST JAMES'S,
LONDON. S.W.1

Telephone
WHITEHALL 6133

Cheques—ECCENTRIC CLUB LTD.

This statement does NOT include any payment received after date shown above.

Chic and Maidie, still at
the top of the bill, during a
television recording of
STV's *Holiday Fanfare*
in the early 60s.
INSERT, a bill from
The Eccentric Club of
which Chic was naturally
a member.

The many faces of Chic in his later years.

16

THE 'WEE CAPTAIN' SCRIPT

With her usual sense of occasion Maidie asked a friend at home in Edinburgh to cut a record of the couple's very first BBC broadcast, thus preserving a tiny moment of history. Compere Eddie Frazer introduced them as 'Another Scots act, and all harmony too, for Chic and Maidie are man and wife. As this is their first broadcast I hope you'll give a particularly warm hand to the unusual comedy duo of "Chic and Maidie" . . .'

With 'Ballin' the Jack' as their introductory music, off they went:

Chic: I met a fellow in Glasgow today. I hadn't seen him for quite a long time. As a matter of fact I hadn't been there for quite a long time, that's the real reason. And he's a steward on board the *Queen Mary.*

Maidie: Oh?

Chic: Yes, I didn't know that at first until he told me, see? And as a matter of fact they carry passengers, he was telling me. I know the boat carries passengers. I *know* that – it helps them to pay their way, you know.

The fellow was talking to me as if he thought I was a fool – I'll need to think that over sometime, aye. And he was talking to me because he could speak and it made it easier for both of us, him talking. So he said, 'Listen I'm a steward on board the *Queen Mary*.' I said, 'You said that before.' He said, 'Well, just in case you missed it' – that goes for the audience too, of course.

Maidie: They'll appreciate that, Chic.

Chic: Be quiet. So this particular passenger he had was Miss Betty Grable and he said one night a peculiar incident happened. The bell rang and he tripped along to Betty Grable's cabin. Hey, *I* would have nipped along to Betty Grable's cabin no matter who rang the bell!

Maidie: Chic!

Chic: What?

Maidie: I'd have been at your back!

Chic: You'd have been there! So he went to Betty Grable's cabin and he said, 'Yes, Miss Grable?' Well, that was her name, and he addressed her as such. Why shouldn't he?

Maidie: No reason, Chic.

Chic: Precisely. He said, 'Yes, Miss Grable. What's the matter?' And she said, 'Well, steward, there's an unusual noise in my

98

	cabin,' He looked all around and found nothing. So he began to leave. No point in him staying in there, you know what I mean.
Maidie:	I know what you mean, Chic.
Chic:	Are you sure? As he stood at the door he said, 'Miss Grable, there's absolutely nothing.' And she said, 'Well, I can assure you there was a noise and it was keeping me off my sleep.' So he said, 'Well, if it occurs again, please ring.' She said, 'I will.' He said, 'Well, that's very good. Please do.' He was quite polite, you know. He was a polite steward.
Maidie:	They're the best kind.
Chic:	Of course they are! So then he went away to wherever he'd been. Wherever he'd been's his own business of course, nothing to do with us. He decided to await further developments. When I say further developments, I mean another ring.
Maidie:	I know you do.
Chic:	Really! So the bell rang again – when I say the bell rang, oh, it's just a wee press. Another fool would pull it up and down! So there he is waiting, you see, he's just waiting because nothing's happening. So the bell rings again and off he goes again to Betty Grable's cabin. He goes through the usual preliminaries. 'Yes, Miss Grable, what is it?' She says, 'That noise has occurred again. It's keeping me off my sleep.' He said, 'What is

the noise like, Miss Grable? Can you describe it?' She said, 'Well, I hardly like to tell you.'

'Och,' he said, 'go on.' And he dug her in the ribs. Well, no he didn't – he'd have been a cheeky steward if he'd done that.

Maidie: He certainly would.

Chic: SILENCE! So she said, 'OK, steward, I'll tell you what it sounds like. It's just like this – "pitter, patter, pitter, patter, *whooch, whooch*".' To which he replied, 'Good heavens.' It *was* quite a nice night as a matter of fact.

Maidie: Was it?

Chic: Yes it was, and stop interrupting. Then he said, 'I think I'll tell the captain about this.' And he and the steward are bent listening. Mind you, I don't really know if they were bent or not. I'm only putting that in myself, because they'd put the lights out.

Maidie: Chic!

Chic: What?

Maidie: He might have been a wee captain.

Chic: He could have been a wee captain. Good! That's good. Here – I wish you'd shut your face! So they're listening – bent or not – and they hear it! Pitter, patter, pitter, patter, *whooch, whooch*. 'On with the lights!' shouts the captain. He is the captain, after all. *He's* not going to put them on with the steward being there. 'On with the lights!' And they look all around and can find nothing. 'Put them out again,' ordered the captain, and they're listening again. At last they hear it – Pitter, patter, pitter, patter, *whooch, whooch*. 'On with the lights!' On go the lights again. So they look all around and now they see it. You know the hot pipes that run along the walls of cabins? They're there to keep the cabin warm, basically.

Maidie: Yes, I know.

Chic: Well, there's a little mouse crawling along one of them. And the pipe's so hot that the mouse is going 'pitter, patter, pitter, patter', then lifting up his little paws and blowing on them: '*Whooch, whooch*'.

17

ALARUMS & EXCURSIONS

It took me 25 years before I realized I was a lousy comedian. By that time I couldn't give it up. I was famous.

•

As I kissed my new girlfriend I suddenly got a lump in my throat. She'd been chewing a pickled onion.

•

The case of the foreign diplomat is coming up next week. It's called an attaché case.

•

This cowboy came riding in on a cloud of dust. No horse, just a cloud of dust.

•

Sylvester won't take his wife out. He says he doesn't care for married women.

•

'Sits Vacant.' That's a good description of our Ron.

•

My grandfather was a genius. He invented a cure for which there was no disease. Unfortunately my grandmother caught the cure.

•

Warning to all ship owners. Never let your dingy dangle in the wake.

•

I've had a few foreign affairs, but none that are current.

•

Instead of 'woof-woof', Blackie the sheepdog goes 'wool-wool'.

•

After driving along the highway at 70 mph, then entering the slow lane, giving perfect hand-signals, and slowing down to 30 mph, the motorist was stopped by police. 'Don't worry, sir,' they assured him. 'There's nothing wrong. We just wanted to compliment you on your perfect driving.'

The driver stared at them glassily and replied, 'You've got to be careful when you're as drunk as I am.'

•

'This shirt will laugh at washing,' the salesman told me. So it did. It came back from the laundry with its side split.

•

I would have become a coroner, only they say you have to take a stiff exam.

When I had Daphne to tea, she was so excited she broke out in suggestive biscuits.

If the present rise in prices continues, the good old days will be last week.

I was always smiling as a baby. I had to, I swallowed a banana sideways.

'Certainly I take exercise,' I told my GP. 'I roll my own cigarettes.'

You know what they say about stamp collecting? Philately will get you nowhere.

We're 18 weeks behind with the rent now, but next week it will all be different. We'll be 19 weeks behind.

I spotted Effie in the pub and could tell right away she had class by the way she ordered a pint of heavy and spat on the sawdust.

Dan's wife never knew whether she was coming or going with him. He kept driving up and down their street in a removal van.

I've a violin that only plays at night. The strings are made from tomcatgut.

•

The hardest jobs for the foreman in the stocking factory were bringing the workers to heel and making them toe the line.

•

I told one of my employees he was going places. Then I fired him just to make absolutely sure.

•

I do my hardest work before breakfast. Getting up.

•

Our neighbours have got stained glass windows. It's these damned pigeons.

•

After the hardback comes the pocket edition. Couldn't they follow up with a pickpocket edition?

•

If the price of jelly babies goes up any further I'm putting in for family allowance.

•

'I'm sorry to see you coming out of that public house,' the vicar told one of his flock. So he went back in.

•

I got this terrible puncture at the fork in the road.

•

I've an extremely skinny bulldog. Well, it used to be a whippet – until it ran into a wall.

•

Jimmy's always had the spirit of rebellion. When he was born and the doctor slapped him, he turned round and slapped him back.

•

If you were a missionary, would you live in a converted house?

•

Chopin's 'Mayonnaise' – lovely for playing in the kitchen.

•

I drew a gun. He drew a gun. I drew another gun. Soon we were surrounded by lovely drawings of guns.

•

My wife painted a civil servant at work and won first prize in a still-life competition.

•

A man and his pal went into a Glasgow bar. 'Give me two pints and two double whiskies,' he said to the bartender. Then he turned to his pal, 'And what'll you have?'

•

'OBE' was the simple message he left outside his hotel door. 'I didn't know you'd been honoured,' said the housekeeper in the morning. 'I wasn't,'

he replied. 'That was my breakfast order – One
Boiled Egg.'

●

'The Plumber's Pipe Band' their card ran, 'for
Water Music with a Difference.'

●

There's a new book out on space travel that's
supposed to be completely out of this world.

●

Note left behind by a sailor: 'Out to launch.'

●

There's an old gardening saying: 'Don't prune
your damsons in September, or your gooseberries
will fall off in the spring.'

●

Being a fishmonger is a sole-destroying job.

●

Sonny celebrated his 21st birthday in prison and
asked if he could have the key of the door.

●

The prisoner in the dock had thrown his mother-
in-law out of a window three floors up. 'That was
dangerous,' the judge admonished him. 'Someone
could have been passing at the time.'

●

His father called Rab the apple of his eye. He did
look decidedly seedy.

●

We called our headmaster Victor Sylvester because of his strict temper.

•

There's always a great game of bar billiards going on at our local. We play with pickled onions.

•

Aggie used to have an hour-glass figure. Now all the sand's run to the bottom.

•

Terry wears a leather jacket, leather boots and leather trousers. If he ever falls off that bike of his they can have him soled and heeled.

•

It wasn't what you'd call a good-looking horse. It looked as if two men were trying to get out of it.

•

This woman had a really slow drawl. By the time she was finished telling you about her past, you were part of it.

•

Why can't they invent sharp-edged aspirins for splitting headaches?

•

Cannibals discovered long ago how best to serve their fellow men.

•

Lenny's beard got caught in the mincer. It's the first time I've ever seen cottage pie with a thatched roof.

•

I called her Sugar. Believe me, she was some lump.

•

Get into yourself to get yourself out of yourself.
Then try to lose yourself.

•

What's the matter, baby? Is my little coconut shy?

•

Oh, the hibiscus is in bloom and the senna is in
pod. All must be right with the world.

•

Did you hear the one about the illegitimate rice
crispie? Snap, crackle, but no pop.

•

Me got him. He got me. We got us. What you got?

•

An old man of ninety-two went to a doctor and
told him he was marrying a girl of eighteen. 'Hold
on just a minute, that marriage could prove fatal,'
the doctor told him. 'Let her die,' the old man
replied.

The medic could see he was determined. Thinking it would take the strain off the old man a bit
he made a suggestion: 'Look, if you've made your
mind up about this, why not take in a lodger as
well?'

Some time later the two men met. 'How's the
marriage going?' the doctor asked.

'Fine,' the worthy replied. 'Just fine. My wife's

expecting.' Smiling, the doctor asked, 'Did you follow my advice and take in a lodger, then?'

'I did that,' said the old geezer. 'And she's expecting as well.'

•

Did you hear about the Eskimo couple who got engaged? On the way to the church they had an argument, so she broke it off.

•

Does a stocking manufacturer see the seamy side of life?

•

I wish her eyes were close to mine, instead of being close to each other.

•

I remember one July during the war General March was leading his army. While crossing the river May the bridge collapsed. It's the only time in history March has fallen in May during July.

•

Two elderly men had been bowlers all their lives, and at sixty-five they had won everything, and played everywhere together. 'Bob, I wonder if they've bowling greens in heaven?' one of them asked.

'Well, Jim, I don't know about that. But let's make a pact that whoever dies first comes back and tells the other.'

Jim died the following week, and Bob waited patiently for a message, but nothing happened for six months. Bob and his wife went on holiday and on their third day at their hotel he went for a walk in a local wood. Suddenly a big deep voice boomed out. 'Hello, Bob.'

'My goodness, it's you, Jim, at last.'

'Yes, Bob, and they have beautiful bowling greens up here. And guess what? You're down for a tournament next week!'

•

Do you know what kind of lighting they used on Noah's ark? Flood lighting.

18

SOMETHING
TO OFFEND EVERYONE – II
by Minnie Ster

A priest, rabbi and minister all had poor parishes in a poverty-stricken county town. Since none of them could afford to buy a car on his own they decided to club together and share the vehicle. The priest blessed it, the minister said a prayer over it, and the rabbi snipped the end off the exhaust pipe.

●

A minister was cycling down a country lane in his parish one day when he passed a little girl walking her dog. 'My, what a pretty wee miss you are,' he declared. 'Thank you,' she replied. 'My name is Lorraine.'

'Really? That's a lovely name. Are you from this district?'

'Yes I am. My daddy has the farm up on the hill.'

'That's very nice. And what's your wee dog's name?'

'Porky.'

'That's an unusual name for a dog. Why do you call it that?'

'Because it interferes with all the pigs on Daddy's farm.'

•

A woman took her twin boys to get christened. 'What are their names?' the minister asked.

'Hitler and Mussolini,' she replied.

'My goodness,' he declared. 'Why is that?'

'Because they're a couple of bastards.'

•

A priest and a minister had joined the Ecumenical Council. The minister invited the priest over to his church to join the service. 'Very nice,' the priest told him. 'I enjoyed that very much. You must come over to my chapel next week.'

After the service the minister said how much he had enjoyed it. 'Oh, no,' said the priest, 'that's not all. It's confession time now. Come into the box with me and I'll show you how it's done.'

As the minister kneeled down with the priest, a voice came from the adjacent confession booth. 'Father, I have sinned. I wish to confess that I have raped five women.'

'Well,' said the priest, 'I want you to say five Hail Marys, five Ave Marias and put 50p in the box.'

A few moments later another voice piped up: 'Father, I have sinned. I wish to confess that I have raped five women.'

'Say five Hail Marys, five Ave Marias and put 50p into the box,' the priest again replied. Then he turned to the minister: 'Look, I've got to nip out to the bathroom. Take over while I'm gone.'

Two minutes later came another voice: 'Father, I have sinned. I wish to confess that I have raped three women.' The minister thought for a moment. 'Well, off you go and rape another two. It's five for 50p this week.'

●

A circus came to town and the acrobat went to the local chapel for confession. After the priest had listened intently and discovered what the chap did for a living, he said, 'My goodness, it's years since I was at a circus. Could you do some tricks for me?'

'Certainly,' said the acrobat, and began to do handstands, then somersaulted up and down the aisle. Just then two old ladies walked into the chapel. 'My God,' one of them declared, 'if that's the new man's idea of penance, I'm off to join the Proddies.'

●

A minister was doing his hospital round, visiting his parishioners in the ward, when one of the ward sisters came up to him: 'Father, would you mind visiting the wee Chinaman at the end of the ward? He's in a bad way.'

The minister found the Chinaman lying in bed wearing an oxygen mask. Leaning over, he asked, 'How are you, my son?' The Chinaman turned red and mumbled at him, waving his arms frantically. 'I don't understand,' the minister told him. 'All I asked was, how are you, my son?'

At this the Chinaman turned deep purple and started a muffled babbling. 'I still can't make you out,' said the minister. In desperation the Chinaman grabbed a pen and paper, wrote something down in Chinese, then turned black and collapsed on the bed dead.

The minister sought out the ward sister. 'I'm afraid the Chinaman has just died,' he told her, 'but before he passed away he wrote me a note. Unfortunately, I don't read Chinese.'

'I do, Father,' said the sister. 'Let me see. Oh, dear God! It reads: "You stupid bastard. You're standing on my oxygen supply!"'

●

A fellow entering a monastery as a nervous monk was told by the abbot he would only be allowed to talk for one minute every five years. After five years he stood up. 'There's not enough salt in the porridge,' he declared, and sat down again.

Another five years passed, and again he stood up and said, 'The porridge still hasn't got enough salt in it.'

After another five years had passed, he stood up for a third time and said, 'Your porridge is still rotten. And I'm leaving.'

'Thank God,' said the abbot. 'You've done nothing but complain since you came here.'

●

A Salvation Army band was playing in the street for about thirty minutes. The bandleader finally asked the crowd, 'What hymn would you like now?' A woman's voice came from the back of the crowd. 'Him with the big drum.'

●

Two priests were on a plane to Rome and halfway there the pilot switched on the intercom. 'Sorry to trouble you, but we have an emergency. Our electrical supply has a fault in it and we may have to make an emergency landing in the sea. Will you please put on your life jackets.' One priest turned to the other. 'We better hear each other's confession before it's too late. I'll go first. I've been a heavy smoker and drinker, and been with nearly every woman, married or single, in my parish.'

The other priest said, 'I wish to confess that I'm an alcoholic and I like little boys.'

Just then the intercom was switched back on and the pilot's voice was heard. 'It's all right now, folks,' he declared. 'The emergency is over.'

At this one priest turned to the other: 'Isn't it amazing the lies you tell when you're scared?!'

•

An abbot strode into the assembly hall every morning and chanted, 'Good morning, brothers,' and all the brothers chanted, 'Good morning, Father,' back at him. One monk was really bored by this, so he decided to have a change, and the next morning when the abbot came in and said, 'Good morning, brothers,' and all the brothers chanted back, 'Good morning, Father,' he chanted, 'Good evening, Father.'

The abbot was really surprised and declared, 'Someone chanted evening!'

•

Jesus turned to St Andrew and St Peter and said, 'The world's in a terrible state. We'll have to go down and perform another miracle.' St Peter said, 'I know! We'll do the walking on water miracle.'

'All right,' Jesus agreed. Down they went on earth and landed on the pier at Saltcoats. After hiring a boat St Peter and St Andrew rowed well out into the water. St Peter said, 'We're far enough out. Try it now.'

Jesus gingerly went overboard and stood in the water, but only for a couple of seconds before falling in. They pulled him into the rowing boat. 'Try it again, Jesus,' said St Peter. But it was to no avail. Jesus sank again.

After they had pulled him into the boat St Andrew said, 'What's wrong, Jesus? It worked so well the last time!'

'Well,' said Jesus. 'Maybe it's these holes in my feet.'

•

A red-hot Orangeman was really hurt and angry at his little boy, who began to flunk all his classes at school. Gradually his marks got worse and worse. Finally he had been expelled from three famous Protestant schools. In great sorrow, the Orangeman sent the boy to a private Roman Catholic school.

After six months had passed the wee boy had perfect attendance, perfect behaviour and had kept himself clean and tidy. By the end of the term his marks had improved a hundred per cent.

The Orangeman was really surprised – and enraged – by this and collared his son one night. 'What's this carry-on?' he asked. 'I send you to good Protestant schools and you mess everything up. Then I send you to this Catholic school and a complete change comes over you.'

'Well, Dad, it's like this,' the boy explained. 'There's a poor bloke been nailed to a big wooden cross ever since I went there. And I don't want to be next.'

•

Three wee boys walking by the river noticed a man drowning. Diving in, they rescued him. 'My sons,' he said when he had recovered, 'I'm a priest in the holy Roman Catholic church, and just to show my gratitude you may have any wish granted. Just ask.'

The first wee boy said, 'Can I get a visit to

Lourdes to pray to keep my family in good health?'

'Granted, my son.'

The second wee boy said, 'I'd like a trip to Rome to visit the Pope.'

'Granted, my son.'

The third wee boy piped up: 'I'd like a state funeral.'

'Dear goodness,' said the priest, 'what a strange request for a child of your tender years. What on earth do you want a state funeral for?'

'Because my father's a red-hot Proddy,' said the wee boy, 'and when he finds out who I saved from drowning, he'll murder me.'

19

TALES OF INVERKIP

One day, while appearing in Inverkip, I went to buy a suit. The shopkeeper told me that the wool was from Scotland, it had been woven in Yorkshire and tailored in London. 'Wonderful,' I thought. 'All these people earning a living out of it – and I haven't even bought it yet.'

I gave the performance of my life at the local Empire that night. 'Oh, God,' I thought as I surveyed the punters, 'my kind of audience – drunks!' I had the feeling that getting a laugh was going to be like finding a virgin in a maternity ward. 'It's very nice to be in front of an audience again,' I told them, 'grim-looking and tight-lipped though you are.'

The pianist who accompanied me was something else. Jimmy Durante was the man who found the lost chord, but this geyser couldn't even have found Jimmy Durante. Some pianists can read music – he couldn't even read the words. He was truly desperate, the kind of young man who would send his mother into space for a publicity stunt, then sell up and move house. Despite his dastardly efforts I managed to finish my act on a musical note. Splinter Lips McMurray they call me, the Man with the Wooden Trumpet.

The audience gave me a big hand. One over each ear.

I then announced that the next act needed no introduction. It was true – they hadn't turned up yet. Then I took a bow. I don't think the fiddler in the orchestra was all that pleased, but I took it anyway. 'Thank you for having me,' I said to the audience, 'and for those who haven't had me yet, be patient.' Then the orchestra faded away, I faded away, the lights faded away, and we tried to find a happy medium.

I went back to my hotel after the show. It was a very high-class hotel. They changed the sheets on the bed every day – from one room to the other. It was a nice hotel, everyone was very nice to me. Even the doorman treated me as an equal. I still felt as out of place as a left-handed violinist in a crowded string section. 'If I telephoned room service,' I wondered, 'would they send me up another room?'

Next morning at breakfast the local temptress chose to sit beside me. 'The name's McFruity,' she told me, sat there in her low-cut boiler suit. 'Nectarine McFruity. Do you see anything you like?'

'No,' I replied, 'although it sounds delicious.'

'Where have you been all my life?' she asked me, completely undeterred by my moving to another table.

'I must have been some place,' I replied.'I've got a whole trunk full of clothes downstairs.'

'Let me gentle you into the day,' she suggested.

'Sorry,' I told her, 'I've got to go. I'm off for my weekly appointment with fear at the Labour Exchange.' I couldn't wait to get away – the water on my knee was beginning to boil!

On my way to the theatre that night I stopped

for a refreshment at the Village Tea Shop. I was intrigued by the sign outside which read, 'Tea. Coffee. Ices. Poison Pen letters a speciality: ask for rates.' Inside I bumped into my agent. He used to be an effervescent kind of fellow, but since he's fallen on hard times his fizz level has dropped considerably. He informed me that I was wanted by a film company to play the important part of an Indian. This was too much! I put my foot down and told him I'd play a *whole* Indian or nothing! 'You're a perfect idiot!' he shouted at me.

'Nothing in life,' I pointed out, 'is perfect.' Then I left him there, crying pitifully into his haggis supper.

Who needs agents anyway? They say that if you haven't got one you'll get diddled. But when you do get an agent, you still get diddled – and pay him ten per cent on top for the privilege!

On this particular visit to Inverkip I could see that the town had been transformed, the *nouveau riche* had moved in. Why, I saw a wee boy playing on the beach with a mink-lined bucket. And they were so used to fur coats in the local bistro that two bears strolled in and ordered lunch and nobody even noticed.

But I digress. I often do when I'm tired. Don't we all! Oh, never mind. I was glad to see the old place looking up. I even went down to inspect the town's latest pride and joy, the new marina. They've still got a long way to go, I found. One of the boats was so old it must have been launched when Long John Silver had two legs and an egg on his shoulder. Oh, well, at least they're trying, I thought. *Very* trying! But you know, I have a great fondness for these Clydeside resorts. Why, just a few years ago I spent a rare day in Largs. I weighed myself twice!

20

SLANG ME A RHYME

Chic's obsession with rhyming slang began shortly after I brought him into show business. We were sitting round the dining room table in lodgings along with the rest of the cast. When one of us wanted the salt they would cry, 'Pass the Willie Galt, please.' (William R. Galt was a Glasgow agent in those days.) Then it would be 'Pass the Tam Reid' (breid) or 'Pass the skip the gutter' (butter). Or 'Pass the fisherman's daughter (water), or 'Pass the Duke of York' (pork).

Chic was new to this and felt excluded from our 'old pro' talk, which to us was just routine. Finally he piped, up, 'Excuse me, could you pass the Campbell Bannerman?'

Everyone looked at him, utterly baffled. 'What's that?' someone finally asked. 'I don't know,' says Chic, looking completely unabashed. 'But it sounds good!' Thereafter he became an ardent devotee of the lingo, even of the variations. 'MacFarlane and Lang' was the 'official' rhyming name for the slang, then this would be abbreviated to MacFarlane (as in 'Can you go the MacFarlane?') For the smartypants among us who want to take it a stage further, MacFarlane became McVitie and Price, or, in the end, just plain 'McVitie'.

I'm glad we've been able to preserve here just a few of Chic's favourites.

Maidie.

I'm taking my King Richard III to the dolly mixtures.
abbreviated to
I'm taking my Richard to the dollies.
meaning
I'm taking my bird to the pictures.

•

We're heid-the-ball off in the jam jar for a currant bun.
abbreviated to
We're heid off in the jam for a currant.
meaning
We're all off in the car for a run.

•

There's a rock and roll in your Rothesay docks.
abbreviated to
There's a rock in your Rothesays.
meaning
There's a hole in your socks.

•

My marzipan's a collie dug. He's away to the cream cookies for a shampoo and set.
abbreviated to
My marzi's a collie. He's away to the cream for a shampoo.
meaning
My man's a mug. He's away to the bookies for a bet.

126

I butt and ben a lads and lassy rub a dub dub.
They've got breid crust on the Dan Dare.
abbreviated to
I butt a lads dub. They've got breid on the Dan.
meaning
I ken a classy pub. They've got sawdust on the
flair.

●

See that wee tailor's vest? He's got nae Davidsons
Mains.
abbreviated to
See that wee tailor's. He's got nae Davidsons.
meaning
See that wee pest? He's got nae brains.

●

Give us a month o' June on your Tommy Morgan,
said the lemon curd.
abbreviated to
Give us a month on your Tommy, said the lemon.
meaning
Give us a tune on your organ, said the bird.

●

My marzipan's elephant's trunk on the Vera Lynn.
abbreviated to
My Marzi's elephant's on the Vera.
meaning
My man's drunk on gin.

●

Rothesay pier! The chucky stane's Lillian Gished
the Uncle Ned!
abbreviated to

Rothesay! The chucky's Lillianed and the Uncle!
meaning
Oh dear! The wean's pissed the bed!

●

I'm West-End toff to my Uncle Ned for a Bo-Peep.
abbreviated to
I'm West-End to my uncle for a Bo.
meaning
I'm off to my bed for a sleep.

●

Catch that Mona Lisa! He's giving ma claes pegs a Rookery Nook.
abbreviated to
Catch that Mona! He's giving ma claes a Rookery.
meaning
Catch that geezer! He's giving my legs a look.

●

My marzipan's lit the flame with a rerr terr of winners and losers.
abbreviated to
My marzi's lit with a rerr of winners.
meaning
My man came hame with a pair of troosers.

●

Yer ima float's craigendorn at the babbit's pooder.
abbreviated to
Yer ima's craigen at the babbit's.
meaning
Yer coat's torn at the shooder.

●

I'll sure-fire bet more Nat King Cole for the Paddy Maguire.

abbreviated to
I'll sure-fire more Nat for the Paddy.
meaning
I'll get more coal for the fire.

●

Have you butter-beaned your Water o' Leith?
abbreviated to
Have you buttered your Water?
meaning
Have you cleaned your teeth?

●

I'll cop a jook in the Jack 'n' Jill, check the home
on the range and visit the J. Arthur Rank.
abbreviated to
I'll cop in the Jack, check the home and visit the
J. Arthur.

meaning
I'll take a look in the till, check the change and
visit the bank.

21

RIPPING RIPOSTES

First sheep: Baaa!

Second sheep: Moo!

First sheep: That should be 'Baaa!'

Second sheep: I know. But I'm trying to learn a second language.

•

Performer: I do bird imitations.

Agent: Really? Do you whistle or sing?

Performer: No. Just eat worms.

•

Michael: Let's meet tonight in Finnegan's bar.

Paddy: Righto. If you don't see me, feel around a bit. The sawdust's pretty deep in there.

•

Jockey: Are you here for a flutter?

Punter: No, we're here to watch the races. Here, is that really a three-year-old horse? It's got grey hair.

Jockey: Yes, it worries a lot.

Punter: Do you always ride sidesaddle?

Jockey: No, the starting gate went up before I could cock my other leg over.

•

Wee boy: Did you know they had Indians up in the Shetlands?

Pal: No.

Wee boy: They do. Shetland Pawnees.

•

Sanny: Dad, there's a Black Maria outside.

Dad: Bring her in, there's no prejudice in here.

•

Dan: I saw a monkey chipping potatoes in a restaurant.

Aggie: Really? Sounds to me like a chip monk.

•

Lola: I'll give you £750 if you'll paint me in the nude.

Gregor: OK, but I'll need to keep my socks on. I'll have nowhere else to put my brushes.

•

Boozer:	These are cute little green ice cubes. Most unusual.
Bartender:	Well, as a matter of fact we ran out of ice. They're frozen peas.

•

Father:	Now boys, off to bed, otherwise Santa won't visit you tonight.
Sons:	Oh no? Who do you think we've got in this sack?

•

Fergus:	What's the first thing you notice about a girl?
Archie:	It all depends whether she's coming or going.

•

Teacher:	Name a fish that likes a lot of sleep.
Pupil:	Kippers.

•

Alex:	Why don't you do something for your country?
Jock:	Like what?
Alex:	Emigrate.

•

Patrick:	Are you a ghost?
Bill:	I'm aghast.
Patrick:	I should have guessed.

133

●

First Artiste:	We had a drink on the manager after the show.
Second Artiste:	Was it good?
First Artiste:	Yes, but a wee bit uncomfortable.

●

| Interviewer: | Have you academic leanings? |
| Sandy: | No, I've just lost the rubber on my left heel. |

●

| Bertha: | I'd like a diamond to match my eyes. |
| Jeweller: | Don't be daft. They haven't yet invented bloodshot diamonds. |

●

| Tam: | I'm working eighteen hours a day. |
| Rosie: | Never mind, a part time job is better than none at all. |

●

| Alex: | I just want to teach my girlfriend right from wrong. |
| Jimmy: | Very worthy. How about you teach her what's right and leave the rest to me? |

●

| Sam: | She keeps all her money in the tops of her stockings. |

Fred: I wish my bank had branches like that.

•

Jamie: I want a pair of crocodile shoes.

Shopkeeper: What size does your crocodile take?

•

Euphemia: Did you miss a step when you fell down those stairs?

Bill: Nope. I hit every single one.

•

Worried Mum: One problem after another. Our young Jimmy's ran away with the circus.

Neighbour: What was your next problem?

Worried Mum: Two weeks later he brought it back with him again.

•

Dad: A fool and his money are soon parted.

Mum: Who got yours?

•

Alasdair: What is there to do at a seaside boarding house that you can't do at home?

Eckie: Remove the sand from your belly button.

Shareen:	I gave my man a lovely going-away present.
Doris:	Where's he going?
Shareen:	He isn't. Unless he takes the hint.

•

First Idiot:	You're an Italian, aren't you?
Second Idiot:	No, I'm not.
First Idiot:	Yes, you are.
Second Idiot:	No, I'm not.
First Idiot:	Yes, you are.
Second Idiot:	Well, if that's the way you want it – fine, I'm Italian.
First Idiot:	I *thought* you were. But here – you don't look it.

•

Comedian:	Did you hear my last broadcast?
Punter:	Yes. And so it should be.

•

Diner:	Waiter, remove this fly from my soup.
Waiter:	Why?
Diner:	I wish to dine alone.

•

Albert:	He's the luckiest man alive.
Egbert:	How?

136

Albert:	Well, for years he was digging his own grave. Then he struck oil.

•

Winthrop:	What are you going to do with the pig?
Sedgwick:	That's not a pig, it's a duck.
Winthrop:	I'm talking to the duck.

•

Alastair:	Do you know algebra?
Colin:	No, I never took foreign languages.

•

Effie:	The astrologer told me to marry a Capricorn.
Pam:	What's a Capricorn?
Effie:	A goat.
Pam:	It'll never work out.

•

Boozer:	This is an extremely large gin and tonic.
Host:	No, it's not. It's a goldfish bowl.
Boozer:	Really? I wondered why the slice of lemon kept leaping out of my mouth.

•

Salesman:	We've got a wonderful line for bald-headed men.

Customer:	What is it?
Salesman:	Bald-headed women.

•

Sadie:	See that man? A lie never passed his lips.
Nora:	Is that so?
Sadie:	Yes, all his life he spoke through his nose.

•

Egbert:	I've come down to London from Glasgow three years running.
Norbert:	Have you ever considered flying?

•

Baby Camel:	Mummy, why have I got two humps?
Mother Camel:	To hold extra water in the desert.
Baby Camel:	Mummy, why have I got hooded eyes?
Mother Camel:	To keep the desert sand out of them.
Baby Camel:	Mummy, why have I got such big feet then?
Mother Camel:	So you don't sink in the desert sand.
Baby Camel:	Well, why the hell are we in Edinburgh Zoo then?

22

CHIC ON MARRIAGE

My wife Betty had a terrible accident when she was born. She lived. She was such an ugly child that when she entered a dark room, the dark screamed. Her mother used to beg her to sleep with her head in the pillow in case she frightened the burglars.

I'm not saying she's odd-looking, but in a lineup she's always picked out from real people. She's got a terrible lumpy skin. Apparently her mother was frightened by sago pudding.

The two of us spent ten wonderfully happy years in Edinburgh, of which we both have warm, nostalgic memories. Then we met each other.

Our romance began as a blind date. 'I'll see you at seven at the top of Waverley Steps,' I told her on the phone. 'How will I know you?' she asked. 'I'll be wearing a yellow handkerchief in my inside pocket and a pair of matching Y-fronts,' I said.

We got married in a very simple ceremony, no fancy trimmings. Even the minister's name was the Rev. Smith. I caused a bit of a sensation by turning up in white tie and tails. No-one had told me about the trousers.

The ceremony was a private affair – just the four of us, me, Betty, the minister and the midwife.

139

We went to London for our honeymoon. Actually, I went on my own, it turned out she'd been before. After the honeymoon we settled down in our new home, where everything was brand-new. I was kept awake all night listening to our contemporary furniture coming unstuck.

No sooner were we married than Betty began to put on an incredible amount of weight. She looked like Jayne Mansfield and Sophia Loren, but all rolled up into one big, ugly, shapeless lump. I'm not saying she was fat, but her belly and her behind had to be given different postal codes. She went on a seafood diet. She only had to see it to eat it.

Oddly enough, she's a great sportswoman, captain of Inverkip's Ladies Mud-Wrestling team, Sumo division. And she's potty about bingo. She had a plaque made to go above our fireplace that read, 'Bless our housey-housey'.

I could see she was very upset when I got home one night. She'd been having a bath in the afternoon – not a pretty sight, no matter what the time of day – when the doorbell rang. 'Who is it?' she bellowed through. 'I'm a blind salesman,' said the man at the door. 'Come in, then,' she yelled, sat there like a landed Great White.

'Where do you want these blinds?' the salesman asked.

Last year I gave her a credit card and she lost it. I haven't reported it, because whoever's found it is spending just a fraction of what she did.

The two of us visited a waxworks the other day. The attendants asked me if I could ask her to keep walking about as they were stocktaking.

You have to be careful what you say to her sometimes. After I told her that black underwear turned me on, she didn't wash my Y-fronts for a month.

You know, I think there's something going on between the milkman and my wife. I sneaked down early to breakfast one morning, crept up behind her and kissed her on the back of her neck. 'We'll only need two pints this morning,' she said. Last week she stayed out all night. When I asked her where she'd been she told me she'd been sleeping with the girl next door. Well, I knew that was a lie – that's where I'd been!

My in-laws are something else. Avoirdupois obviously runs in the family. Her mother's the fattest woman I've ever seen. The only thing she can buy ready-made is a handkerchief. She's so fat that if she wants to turn over in bed she has to get out and come back in again. Another fatty is her Aunt Fanny. She's got so many double chins that when I kiss her I get lost in the pleats.

I came home one afternoon recently and found my wife swinging our cat round and banging it up against the wall. 'What's the idea of treating the cat like that?' I asked. 'Well,' she said, 'when you were playing cards with your mates last night I heard you say there were a couple of pounds in the kitty.'

I'll say one thing for her. She's a great cook. Her lemon meringue pie is a poem in a pan. And when she makes porridge I always ask for a second slice. Seriously, though, I miss my wife's cooking. Whenever I can. She makes things so heavy we're the only house in the street with a bow-legged stool.

'I'm homesick,' I told her the other day. 'Don't be silly,' she replied, 'this is your home.'

'I know,' I said, 'and I'm sick of it.'

Mind you, she sticks to me through all the

troubles I'd never have been in if I hadn't met her in the first place. They say you should drown your sorrows. The trouble is I can never get her near enough the water. She says I'm effeminate. Besides her, I am!

Our son's a really bright boy. When he grows up he's going to start his own country and apply for foreign aid. When we were expecting our second baby I had to break the news to him. 'A stork is going to fly round in circles,' I said, 'and drop a baby down the chimney right into your mother's bed.'

'I hope it doesn't frighten the life out of her,' he replied. 'She's having one herself.'

He's a cheeky wee beggar! I call him Rover, I'd always wanted a dog. The other day I heard there was one going cheap. Funny, I always thought they went woof-woof.

'Where's my tea?' I asked my wife last night. 'I'm keeping it warm for you,' she replied. 'I threw it on the fire.'

One of these days I swear I'm going to tell her who's the boss. I'm going to say, 'You're the boss!'

'How's your good wife?' a pal asked me the other day. 'I don't know,' I told him. 'I've only got the one.' In all honesty I do have a warm spot for the wife. I just wish she'd go there.

When I got home last night she was just cleaning a mud pack off her face. When she was finished I asked her what it was all about. 'I've been taking a course of beauty treatment,' she explained. 'It comes in five stages.'

I looked at her disdainfully. 'What stage have you reached?' I enquired. 'Stage four,' she proudly replied, 'I've only got one more treatment to go.'

'By God,' I said. 'It must be a pip!'

Well, you know what they say – first there's the

engagement ring. Then the marriage ring. Then the suffering.

Just think, though. If it wasn't for marriage, husbands and wives would have to fight with strangers.

They say marriage is a lottery, but I don't go along with that. In a lottery, you can win.

23

SOMETHING
TO OFFEND EVERYONE – III
by Rab Innical

The three wise men went into the stable at Bethlehem. One stood on the end of a rake and it came up and hit him in the eye. 'Oh, Jesus Christ,' he yelled.

Mary looked up. 'My, that's a lovely name for the baby,' she said. 'And to think we were going to call him Willie!'

•

A drunk walked up to the ticket office in Glasgow Central station and bought a ticket for Ayr. He staggered up to Platform One singing 'Star O' Rabbie Burns' and the ticket inspector told him, 'Sorry, wrong platform. Try Platform Nine.' Still singing the 'Star O' Rabbie Burns', the drunk staggered to Platform Nine. There the ticket inspector told him, 'The Ayr train has been diverted to Platform Twelve.' Still giving 'Star O' Rabbie Burns' laldie, he got to Platform Twelve and fell on to the train. Unfortunately, he had sat next to a Wee Free minister. 'You drunken, evil man,' the minister berated him. 'Do you know you're on the road to hell?'

'Oh, dear God, is this no murder?' said the drunk. 'I'm in the wrong train again!'

•

A wee Glasgow man jumped on to the London train as it was moving off and at last found a seat beside a priest. 'Hullo rerr. How's it gawn? Here, dae ye know that ye've got yer collar oan the wrang way roon'?'

'I'm a father, my good man,' the priest explained. 'So am I,' said the worthy 'I've seven of them, five boys and two girls. How about you?'

With a beatific smile the priest replied, 'I'm the father of thousands.'

'My Goad, it's no yer collar ye should have oan back tae front. It's your troosers.'

•

Just before the start of a horse race a punter saw a priest sprinkle water over a horse. To his astonishment it won at 4 to 1. For the next six races he watched the priest at the starting stalls sprinkle one of the horses with water – and in each case the horse won. When the time came for the last race the punter decided to get in on the act. This time he watched carefully as the priest poured water over a horse, then put every penny he had on it to win.

Halfway through the race the horse dropped down dead. The punter turned to the priest. 'What happened there?' he asked. 'You put water on all the other horses and they won, but this one dropped dead.'

'I take it you're not a Roman Catholic?' said the priest.

'What the hell's that got to do with it?' asked the punter.

'Well, you obviously can't tell the difference between blessing a horse and giving it the last rites.'

●

A priest was walking through a little market town some miles from his country parish on his day off. He felt a bit hungry, so he went to a small restaurant in a back street. He ordered steak, which he wanted not too well done. After the meal he thanked the restaurateur and said how much he'd enjoyed the steak. 'Thank you, father,' said his host. 'Next time you're in just ask for a bloody steak and I'll know it's you.' Three weeks later he was having another day off and happened to mention to his bishop he was going to visit the little market town with the nice restaurant. 'That's a place I've never been,' said the bishop. 'Do you mind if I join you?'

The priest took the bishop to the restaurant and said to the waiter, 'Could you give us two bloody steaks, please.' At this the bishop exclaimed, 'Oh, I love this informality. Could we have two bloody great helpings of chips as well, please?'

●

Two Irish navvies were digging a trench outside the local brothel. Pat turned to Mick. 'That's a terrible place. Look at all those brazen, half-naked hussies.'

After a while they spotted a minister sneak round a corner, look around to make sure nobody was watching, and enter the brothel. 'Is that not terrible, Pat?' Mick declared. 'A man of God! But what else can you expect of these Protestants?'

Later they watched as a rabbi furtively made his way into the brothel.

'Did you see that, Mick?' said Pat. 'A rabbi too! Still, I never did trust a man with a beard.'

After a while a car drove into the alley beside the brothel and a priest went in a side entrance. 'Would you look at that, Patrick,' said Mick admiringly. 'It's a brave man going in to reform these unholy sluts.'

'Yes, Michael. And just think of the confessions the poor man will have to listen to as well!'

•

A little Jewish boy was always being told by the rabbi that if he thought evil, dirty thoughts, he would turn into stone. One day he was on holiday in London. Walking through Soho, he slipped in the back door of a strip club and watched for five minutes before running out the front door screaming.

The worried doorman grabbed him and asked what was wrong. 'My rabbi said that if I had dirty thoughts I would turn into stone,' said the wee boy. 'And it's started!!'

24

THE SHOOTING OF DAN McGRUE

A bunch of cowpokes were bumming for booze
    in the Thingummyjig Saloon,
The ragtime guy got a kick in the eye and beat
    out a ragtime tune,
In the back of the bar playing blind man's buff
    was Dangerous Dan McGrue,
And doing the shimmy with Old Scotch Jimmy
    was the lady known as Lou.
In the street outside it was fifty below, at least it
    was more or less,
When out of the night there staggered a sight, with
    a face like an officers' mess,
In Oxford bags, all covered in rags, with twelve
    months' dirt on his skin,
No-one could trace the stranger's face, he'd his
    whiskers outside in.
We could tell by the stubble he was looking for
    trouble, then he pinched another man's beer,
As he tilted his chin the booze ran in and he
    wished us a Happy New Year.
Sat at the piano he removed his bandana and
    played like a man possessed,
As he plunked the keys with his hands and knees
    the sparks flew out of his vest.

149

Were you ever out in the great unknown when the tram was five minutes late?

Have you ever felt your head being crushed like tripe on an empty plate?

Did you ever feel the navvy's boot as it batters you under your eye?

Have you ever been kissed by the factor's clerk? Well, you know what it is to die.

Then the stranger rose and blew his nose and shouted, 'Prepare for the worst!'

He ordered a short and gave a loud snort saying, 'Women and children first!

There's something I want to tell you, and my words are both false and yet true,

There's someone here with another man's wife and that man is Dan McGrue!'

We heard a shout, the lights went out, and a shot rang through the room,

Then he heard a bell and someone yell, a scream and then a boom.

Filled up with booze till it ran from his shoes lay Dangerous Dan McGrue,

And wearing the breeks of the man from the creeks was the lady known as Lou.

25

CHIC'S CHAT

When the first Chic's Chat went ahead on the BBC in the 70s, the listening public were treated to a unique record programme. Apart from boasting some excellent music – more often than not selected with daughter Annabelle's help – Chic's scripts were, not unexpectedly, stamped with his own unmistakable style. This is how the first one ran, with Chic playing all the parts except for Alastair, the announcer:

Andrew Yule

Announcer: When I saw Chic earlier this morning he looked very dressy indeed as he was led down from the horsebox.

Chic (*threateningly*): *Alastair!*

Announcer: You see, Chic's voice broke when he was six. His father knelt on his windpipe.

Cue: Programme's signature tune ('It's A Sin To Tell A Lie', by Somethin' Smith and the Redheads)

Chic (*over music*): Alastair, can I have a word with you before you go? In your own time, of course, and at your own pace.

Announcer: Of course, dear boy.

Chic: You know, I don't know where you get all this stuff you say about me.

Announcer: Well, you write the scripts, dear boy.

Chic: Really? It sounds so different when you read it.

Announcer: Don't worry, Chic. We all love you – it says here.

Chic (*as tune ends*): Well, all I can say is, just be sure it's true. You know, I'm fed up being asked what's worn under my sporran. Maybe see-through sporrans are the answer? By the way, Alastair, that's a nice dog you've got there. What's its name?

Announcer: Chocolate.

Chic: Why do you call him Chocolate?

Announcer: Because he's always round trees! No, don't bend down to touch him, Chic. He's got a new collar and he's slipped it twice today. See – I told you. He's gone! What'll I do?

Chic: Don't worry, I'll whistle on him.

Cue: 'Whistler and His Dog' (Instrumental)

Chic (*as music ends*): Did you know there was crowd trouble at Fir Hill last week? Apparently they had to call the police to force them in! Oh, your dog's back. And look what he's doing!

Announcer: Don't put your hand in his mouth like that.

Chic: Put it *in*? I'm trying to get it *out*!

Cue: Hospital noises. (Patients screaming, sound of legs being sawn off, etc.)

Sister: This little boy won't take his medicine, doctor.

Doctor: Give him a spoonful of sugar.

Cue: 'Spoonful Of Sugar' (Julie Andrews)

Patient: What happened to the fellow in the next bed, doctor?

Doctor: He passed away.

Patient: Oh well, that's life!

Cue: 'That's life' (Frank Sinatra)

As music ends: Fish and chip shop: sound of fish frying, chips sizzling.

Chic: Any hot peas, Tony?

Tony: Nae hotta peas. The lasta time I

153

	hada hotta peas, wan of the boys hadda pea-shooter. He scooted pease down the gramophone and choked Sir Harry Lauder.
Chic:	That must have been some-a-time ago, Tony.

Cue: 'Summertime' (Sarah Vaughan)

Tony (*as music ends*): Yes, wee boy?

Wee boy:	Ah want chips.
Tony:	Alrighta sonny – there's your chips. Whit dae ye want on toppa the chips – sot and peppa and vinegar?
Wee boy:	No.
Tony:	You no want sot and peppa and vinegar?
Wee boy:	No.
Tony:	What do ye want on toppa the chips?
Wee boy:	A fish.
Chic:	Bueno Sera, Tony.

Cue: 'Bueno Sera' (Louis Prima)

Headmaster (*as music ends*): We've talked about the Stone Age and the Bronze Age. Now tell me about another age.

Pupil (*timidly*): The Sausage.

Headmaster: Oh no, I hardly think so. That's cheatin'.

Cue: 'Your Cheatin' Heart' (Hank Williams)

Announcer (*as music ends*): There's a fellow having a spot of trouble with his amplifier in the studio next door, Chic. Is it all right if he practises in here?

Chic: Sure, tell him to be my guest.

Cue: 'Heartbreak Hotel' (Elvis Presley)

Chic (*over closing*): That was young Elvis's first and only hit. I wonder what happened to the laddie? I once heard that he opened a dry cleaners next to a church. Obviously he believed that cleanliness was next to godliness! Next week we're going to have 'Music in Miniature' presented by Wee Georgie Wood. Well, never mind. Sometimes we're high, sometimes we're low, sometimes we're at our peak. I'll be here if you'll be there. See you all next week!

26

GIDDY LIMITS – II

Young Alec chasing that girl along the beach is like a dog chasing a motorcycle. Once he catches it he doesn't know what to do with it.

•

I was knocked over by a woman driver twice in one day – once forward, and once in reverse while she was apologizing.

•

I was £2 short in my wages last week and went to complain. 'You didn't say anything last week when we overpaid you by £5,' they said. 'I can forgive one mistake,' I told them, 'but not two!'

•

I won't say I'm a slow developer, but our teacher was quite pleased to have someone her own age in the class to talk to.

•

She was a gay young thing. Everyone drank champagne from her slipper. Then she had to take early retirement, suffering from chronic mildew of the feet.

•

I knew there was money around as soon as I visited the new neighbours. There were grapes on the sideboard and nobody was ill.

•

There were so many bikinis on the beach the other day the tide refused to go out.

•

'If you're not careful,' my brother told me, 'you'll grow up into one of those people our parents warned us about.'

•

The waiter asked me if I'd like anything else to follow. 'The blonde at the next table,' I told him.

•

Mortimer's a stamp collector, but not a very good one. He's already three weeks behind on his National Health.

•

Terence was a drinking man and died peacefully. We had to beat his liver to death, though.

•

The reason Arab women put a camel in the pie dish is to keep the crust up.

•

One of our neighbours took an overdose of cocoa. Now he's throughly browned off.

•

This fellow had such a marvellous mouthful of gold that the insurance company told him he had to sleep with his head in the safe before they'd give him full cover.

•

Fiona had a lovely dress that came right down to her ankles. I wish I'd been there when it came down.

•

Have you heard about the latest things in men's clothing? Women.

•

If her boiler suit had been cut any lower the girl in the downstairs flat could have worn it.

•

When Kojak has a shave, where does he start?

•

Lourdes is fine, but what you gain in being cured you lose in seasickness on the way back.

•

My brother's got a new job with the Tax Department as a pickpocket. Well, they say it saves them a lot of paperwork.

•

Jimmy didn't mind his wife leaving him, but it was a bit much when he went home to his mother and found her trying to rub her name off his birth certificate.

•

He's a good athlete, but if the police catch him he's for the high jump.

●

British Rail had a go-slow recently. If they hadn't advertised it, nobody would have noticed.

●

The bride wore lemon. The bridegroom was a sucker.

●

It's a changing world. Even Hollywood stars are feeling the pinch. They're keeping their wives for another twelve months.

●

My father was a simple man, my mother was a simple woman. You see the result standing in front of you. A simpleton.

●

What is the tyre industry doing about inflation?

●

No wonder she's an unsuccessful witch. Her spelling mistakes are terrible.

●

I feel like a mosquito in a nudist colony. I know what I want to do, but I don't know where to begin.

●

The local council decided to watch the picture another twice before banning it to the general public.

•

At last a magician with an original trick. He saws the lady in half and then puts her in a box.

•

I know a local sword dancer. He often limps around for a chat.

•

English master Mr Page says he's going to stop chatting up young girls. He's turned over a new leaf apparently. It's young boys now.

•

I never give women a second thought. My first covers everything.

•

My sister's got a great eye for men. She uses the other one for reading.

•

When there was a fire in the chorus girls' dressing room it took five minutes to put the fire out and four hours to get the firemen out.

•

In her little bikini Esther looked like a cigar with two bands.

•

When the tattooed lady and the Indiarubber man got together, he rubbed out half of her United Nations.

•

A chap fell out of a ten-storey building and lived. How? He fell out of the ground floor.

●

A chap fell out of ten-storey building. As a crowd gathered round a policeman asked him, 'What happened?'

'I don't know,' he replied. 'I just got here.'

●

We had a streaker down our way last week. He hadn't got twenty yards before he had three proposals.

●

It was so cold in the theatre dressing room that when I opened the wardrobe my jacket and trousers had my overcoat on.

●

My father had a single tooth in the middle of his mouth. He said it was for central eating.

27

CHIC'S PHILOSOPHICAL GEMS

What use is happiness? It can't buy you money.

•

If the new army recruit looks at my daughter and tries to kiss her, I'd make him a private. If he asks for her name and number, I'd make him a military policeman. If he rings his mother up and asks what to do, he's perfect material for a second lieutenant.

•

Colour television? I won't believe it until I see it in black and white.

•

There are three other things beside sex. Nothing you'd want, of course.

•

I made a stupid mistake last week. Come to think of it, did you ever hear of someone making a clever mistake?

•

Often the best way to get rid of a temptation is to yield to it.

•

He who hesitates is lost. So is she who doesn't.

•

Never start an argument with people whose views you do not share.

•

Marriage brings music into your life. Unfortunately, you've got to play second fiddle.

•

If at first you don't succeed, try, try, try again. Then quit.

•

When one barber cuts another barber's hair, have you ever wondered who does the talking?

•

Driving a hearse has its compensations. You're never bothered with back-seat drivers.

•

Are men smarter than horses? Not really. You don't get horses betting on men.

•

Income tax men drive you to drink. Then they increase the duty on drink.

•

My idea of loaded dice – playing snap with a stutterer.

•

Never a truer word spoken – there's no bones in a bag of tripe.

•

Being born outside Matlock is better than being born outside wedlock. But only just.

•

Confucius he say, 'When old friend come to you for loan, look for new friend.'

•

It's a small world, but I wouldn't want to paint it.

•

If something's neither here nor there, where the hell is it?

•

Why can't they raise hens on stilts for people who like scrambled eggs?

28

TALES OF THE UNHINGED

Driver:	Can you fix my car? There's water in the carburettor.
Mechanic:	Sure I can. Where is your car?
Driver:	In the Clyde.

•

Daphne:	Has your boyfriend anything to do with UNO?
Effie:	He never thinks about anything else.

•

Agnes:	If you were half a man you'd take me to the circus.
Dick:	If I was half a man I'd *be* in the bloody circus.

•

Dan:	If everybody went around telling lies, where would we be?
Archie:	In Parliament.

•

Helen: What do you think of Red China?

Bella: It's nice on a white tablecloth.

•

Reverent Worshipper: I hear the minister's giving a sermon this week on the milk of human kindness.

Irreverent Worshipper: I hope it's condensed.

•

Dad: Doctor, my boy eats grapes.

Doctor: Nothing wrong with that.

Dad: Yes, but he eats them off the wallpaper.

•

Boss: My employees have no problem with money.

New Accountant: How's that?

Boss: I don't give them enough.

•

Elaine: Here comes that boy you fancy, Mabel.

Mabel: I'll drop my hanky, that'll make him stop. Oh, dear, I've come out without one. What else can I drop?

•

| Eck: | Have you heard the joke about Rothesay? |
| Nick: | Yes. It's a Bute. |

•

Daniel:	Do you want to come to the disco on Friday?
Florence:	I can't. I'm getting married on Friday.
Daniel:	How about Saturday?

•

Maisie:	My son thinks he's a chicken.
Hattie:	Why don't you get him taken away?
Maisie:	We would, but we need the eggs.

•

Wee boy:	I'm afraid I'll have to put the cat out.
Dad:	Why?
Wee boy:	It's on fire.

•

Jimmy:	You should have seen my wife's face when I brought round the babysitter last week.
Tam:	What was wrong with that?
Jimmy:	Only that we don't have a baby.

•

First wee boy: My uncle watches TV nude, only wearing a bowler hat. He says nobody visits him nowadays since the telly came in.

Second wee boy: What's the bowler hat for, then?

First wee boy: He says somebody might.

Second wee boy: Does he *ever* get dressed?

First wee boy: Only when he's frying sausages.

•

Rab: Quick, grab that pram.

Cathie: But that isn't our baby.

Rab: Don't argue. It's a far better pram.

•

Stu: I only work when trade calls me.

Bill: Is that often?

Stu: Not really. I'm a snow shifter in the summer and a flypaper salesman in the winter.

•

Neil: We've just had a tragedy in our family.

Dan: What's that?

Neil: My brother's joined the police force.

•

Rob: Look at that gorgeous girl on the beach.

Bob: Is that a bikini she's wearing, or is it a birthmark?

•

Sammy: You're not giving your new girl-friend much encouragement, Hamish.

Hamish: I'm fanning the flames of desire with the bellows of indifference.

•

Gregory: That's a very obedient dog you've got there.

Tam: Isn't it? When I say 'heel', it bites my heel.

•

Tosh: My wife and I have had a falling-out.

Ken: Why?

Tosh: I don't think she likes the holiday brochure I gave her for North Vietnam.

•

May: Did you see the Dardanelles when you were on holiday?

Irene: See them? My dear, we had dinner with them every night.

•

| Sean: | I've been a foreman now for four-teen years. |
| Kevin: | That's a helluva long time to be idle. |

●

| Husband: | I've got to get something to keep the household bills down. |
| Wife: | Have you considered a heavy paperweight? |

●

| Wife: | Did you ask for a rise today? |
| Husband: | No, I forgot about it in all the excitement of getting the sack. |

●

Jenny takes her boyfriend to meet her granny, who is somewhat deaf.

Granny (*shouting*): Has the boy got a good job then?

Jenny (*into Granny's ear trumpet*): He's a poulterer, Gran.

Granny:	Eh?
Jenny:	He's a POULTERER.
Granny:	EH?!?
Jenny:	He's a PHEASANT PLUCKER!
Granny:	Aye, he seems like quite a nice fellow.

29

SO MANY QUESTIONS –
SUCH DAFT ANSWERS!

Hitchhiker: Is your car licensed?

Driver: Of course it is.

Hitchhiker: Good, I'll have a gin and tonic
                with lots of ice and lemon, please.

•

Bella: My boyfriend slings a piece of
                rope around my neck and drags
                me after him. Is he serious?

Daphne: No, he's just stringing you along.

•

Milkmaid: Why has this milking stool only
                got three legs?

Farmer: Because the cow's got the udder.

•

Customer: Is that ice cream pure?

Cafe owner: As pure as the girl of your
                dreams.

Customer:	In that case, just give me a packet of fags.

•

Harry:	Shall we join the ladies?
Paddy:	Why? Are they coming apart?

•

Mark:	Oh, it's lovely to see a coal fire again.
Abie:	If you're still here tomorrow night we'll light it for you.

•

Dexter:	Hello. I didn't recognize you clean-shaven.
Sammy:	But I'm always clean-shaven.
Dexter:	And you used to be taller, around six foot two. Now you're only five foot four. Never mind, it's nice to see you again, Dooley.
Sammy:	Just a moment. My name isn't Dooley.
Dexter:	Oh, you've changed your name as well?

•

Rick:	When I last saw you weren't you in the Military Police?
Nick:	Not in, exactly. Between.

•

Greg:	Let's get married.
Peg:	That's impossible. I can't stand your face.
Greg:	Och, I know, but I'll be at work all day.

•

Lily:	I'm in love. I've all the symptoms. I'm off my fodder, eating like a bird.
Mary:	You'll only make yourself cheep.

•

Aggie:	Is your new boyfriend really a man of substance?
Peggy:	Yes, he only uses disposable doilies the once.

•

Neil:	I've long admired you from afar.
Annie:	Fine, that's about the right distance.

•

Wee boy:	Don't keep me in the dark all day, Dad.
Dad:	I can't think of a better place to keep you, son.

•

Diner:	Are you a head waiter?
Waiter:	Yes, sir.

175

Diner: Well, serve me ahead of the others.

•

Mother: What a sweet little boy. Where did he come from?

Student: Medical school. Third jar on the left.

•

Teacher: Who is it that climbs down trees, but never up?

Wee boy: A paratroooper.

•

Mac: I can't tell you how pleased I am.

Eck: Why?

Mac: Because I'm not a bit pleased.

•

Reformed punter: Gambling can be stamped out if we all stick together.

Unreformed punter: You're right. I'd lay odds of 6-4 we'll succeed.

•

Mick: Have you brought your bag with you?

Tony: No, the wife's on night shift this week.

•

First Idiot: Hello, stranger.

Second Idiot: Howdy, stranger.

First Idiot: Are you a stranger, stranger?

Second Idiot: Yes, I'm a stranger, stranger.

First Idiot: You're a mighty strange stranger, stranger.

Second Idiot: Oh, *belt up*!

●

Peter: Wullie loved his dog so much.

Sam: But didn't he used to kick it?

Peter: Yes, but he always took his tackety boots off first.

Sam: We had a dog ourselves once, a dachshund. But it met its end walking round trees.

●

Animal lover: We've put a bell round our cat's neck, so we always know where it is.

Animal hater: Why not just stick it in a drawer instead?

●

Billy: Your daughter was very honest with me. She told me all her faults.

Ian: That's impossible. You were only with her a month.

First Punter: Good God, my horse seems to be running backwards.

Second Punter: Don't worry, you've backed it each way.

•

First farmer: How many sheep have you, Farmer Brown?

Second farmer: I don't know. Every time I try to count them I fall asleep.

•

Jess: I decided to get married at four o'clock in the afternoon.

Robin: Why so late?

Jess: I figured that if it didn't work out, at least the whole day wouldn't be wasted.

•

Agnes: Did you hear about Mrs McAllister going to jail for plucking a turkey?

Dinah: No. How come?

Agnes: She plucked it off a butcher's counter.

•

Sam: Do you know the penalty for bigamy?

Dick: Aye. *Two* mothers-in-law.

First high-wire walker: Could you work without a net?

Second high-wire walker: My dear! My hair would be all over the place.

•

Stu:	My wife always kisses me when I come home from the pub.
Dan:	Is that affection?
Stu:	No, investigation.

•

First wee boy: My dad hasn't had a haircut for ten years.

Second wee boy: Is he eccentric?

First wee boy: No, bald.

•

First scientist: When are you letting the rocket off?

Second scientist: Between twelve and one during the launch hour.

•

Sanny:	Tomato Bobby then call him.
Dave:	Why?
Sanny:	Because he's always in the glass-house.

•

Jock: I know a sensible orchestra con-
                 ductor who leads the band with
                 his elbows.

John: How does that make him sen-
                 sible?

Jock: It enables him to keep his fingers
                 in his ears.

●

First constable: There's mice in the police station.

Second constable: That clinches it. We'll definitely
                 have to bring back the cat.

●

Neighbour: Do you believe in free speech?

Ernest: Certainly.

Neighbour: Good. You won't mind if I use
                 your phone then.

●

First wee boy: My dad went to the police about
                 the threatening letters he's been
                 getting.

Second wee boy: How did he get on?

First wee boy: They said they couldn't do any-
                 thing about it. The letters were
                 from the Inspector of Taxes.

30

TALES OF CHIC

At the outset of their career Maidie (née Dickson) started a scrapbook of press cuttings she could wave under the noses of bookers and agents. They still managed to get the billing wrong, as at the Edinburgh Palladium where they were listed as 'Maidie and Chic Dickson – The Long and the Short of It'.

The last straw for Chic was when they left the theatre one night and someone observed, 'Look, there's big Maidie – and that must be wee Chic, the accordionist!' From then on he vowed it would be Chic and Maidie – in that order – and preferably with Murray as the surname.

•

As a result of a friendship that Chic struck up with young Wullie Woodburn, a player he had much admired over the years, he was introduced to the rest of the Rangers football team and often invited into the enclosure at their games. Soon he was a guest entertainer at many of their dinners, where his saying of grace became a Rangers institution:

'Oh, Lord, heap blessings on the soup,
Heap blessings on the stovies,

Heap blessings on the popes and jews,
The moslems and jehovies,
Heap blessings on all gathered here,
On absent friends and strangers,
And if You've any blessings left,
For Christ's sake, *bless the Rangers!'*

●

In 1983 Chic's grandson Douglas found himself the beneficiary of Chic's freely flowing milk of human kindness. 'Let's fix a date,' Chic declared. 'We'll go out together and get that BMX bike you've been on about.'

On the appointed day torrential rain was falling in Edinburgh. Even young Douglas suggested putting the expedition off until the weather cleared. Maidie agreed, saying it would just be a misery. Chic would have none of it. 'A wee drop of rain never hurt anybody,' was his verdict, so off they went.

As Maidie drove through the rain she could hear Chic begin to interrogate Douglas in the back seat. 'Have you got a chain for the bike yet?' His grandson looked puzzled. 'A chain?' he echoed. 'Why Grandad, I haven't got the bike yet!'

'You'll need a chain though,' Chic worried. 'You can't leave the bike in the Grassmarket or anywhere else in Edinburgh unless it's properly chained up. We'll need to attend to that at the same time.'

'Yes, Grandad.' replied the perplexed youngster.

'Are you coming in?' Chic asked Maidie when they had arrived at the chosen shop. 'No, I'll just sit here in the car while you do your business,' Maidie replied. She watched as Chic and Douglas ran through the rain. Douglas's face as he left the

car was a picture – he could scarcely believe h
was about to get the BMX he had longed for.

An hour passed and there was no sign of them.
Maidie was parked safely enough and kept an eye
on the store as much as visibility would permit.
Another hour passed and still there was no sign.
Meantime, the rain continued relentlessly.

She was just nodding off to sleep when she
heard frantic scrabbling at the car door, waking
her up with a jolt. 'Open up. We're getting
soaked!' Chic yelled.

As they bundled in, Maidie studied their faces.
Chic looked very cross and young Douglas
seemed on the point of tears. 'Did you get the
bike?' she asked.

'Obviously not!' snapped Chic, abandoning in
an instant his air of benevolent grandad. 'That
miserable bugger! All I wanted was a 25% discount, but he won't budge. Anyway, *nil
desperandum*. I'm pretty sure I can get the
bike cheaper in Glasgow. Take us to Waverley
station, Maidie, and I'll take the boy through with
me.'

Maidie knew better than to argue and drove off,
glancing occasionally in the rear mirror at the
distracted Chic and the disconsolate Douglas in
the back seat. Because of the rain their progress
was slow. When they finally arrived and Maidie
had parked, Chic exploded again. 'Is this as near
as you can get?' he demanded to know. 'It's
bloody well *pouring* outside.'

Maidie took a deep breath. 'It's as close as I can
get without actually mounting the tracks,' she
replied.

'No need for sarcasm,' Chic retorted, making no
move to leave. Wee Douglas meantime just sat
there with his chin balanced on his fist. 'Phone me

nen you get back and I'll come and pick you up,' Maidie offered.

'No need,' Chic replied finally. 'I'm having second thoughts. We may not be going. I think I'll go back and take another crack at that bampot here first. He'll be running scared by now, thinking we're well away.' (Despite her growing feeling of tension, Maidie permitted herself a smile at Chic's use of the Americanism.)

As their tracks were retraced she could feel the old familiar knot forming in her stomach that Chic always produced. 'Feartie cat, feartie gowk,' she thought. Love him as she did, she was able to analyse the symptoms he produced – worry that his temper might escalate, that once again any botch-up would be 'all her fault', but most of all concern for Douglas, whose BMX dream was rapidly fading.

As they made to leave the car again, Maidie whispered to her grandson, 'If you get the bike, for God's sake make sure you get the chain as well!'

Chic gave her a final glare before he dashed with his grandson through the rain and disappeared for the second time into the bicycle shop.

One and a quarter hours elapsed before the two appeared. By this time the rain was easing up and the sky was brightening. Chic was positively aglow. 'Open the boot, darling,' he called out. 'Just wait till you see this – it's an absolute beauty!'

Douglas's face was wreathed in smiles as he watched the men from the shop carry the gleaming BMX out to the car. Suddenly, as if someone had pressed a button, the rain stopped completely and a watery sun flickered out. Heading for home, Maidie felt the tension lift. 'I could go a fish supper now,' Chic declared, 'to round off the day, as were.'

'Did you get the discount you wanted?' Maidie finally summoned up the courage to ask.

'I did,' Chic replied, beaming. 'And *two* chains thrown in as well!'

•

Top BBC producer Ian Christie had asked Chic to be a guest on one of the annual 'Children in Need' shows, being transmitted from the BBC studios in Aberdeen.

Chic readily agreed and turned up on the day dripping wet in his bunnet, a very old and scruffy raincoat and a Fine Fare plastic bag containing his assorted sundries. 'What am I to do, what'll I wear?' Chic wanted to know as he stood there dripping away in front of Ian.

An evening suit routine had been planned, but Ian couldn't take his eyes off Chic as he was. 'What you've got on is just perfect,' he said. Chic just stared at him. 'Are you taking the piss, Ian?'

'No, I'm not, Chic. Can't you see it – you're just in out of the rain, you're not stopping, the plastic bag and all that . . .'

'Could you be trying to tell me something, Ian?'

'Yes I am, that I think it'll be a scream.'

Ian could see Chic's personal computer working away at the suggested image and was relieved as a broad smile creased his old friend's face.

'So do I,' Chic declared, 'and it couldn't be for a better cause. But it will be more like "Comedian in Need" than "Children in Need"!'

•

Bernie Alderston was an old friend with whom Chic constantly kept in touch. After his original oble in the hotel business with Maidie, Chic always had a hankering to repeat the experience. He came to see Bernie one day in his friend's official capacity as chief executive at an Edinburgh brewery. After spending twenty minutes on Bernie's telephone calling all over the country, Chic got down to business. There was a small hotel, it seemed, up for sale in Coldstream. Would Bernie come down with him to look it over?

As far as Bernie was concerned Coldstream was a nice enough town, but hardly the teeming metropolis Chic was making it out to be. He nonetheless drove from Edinburgh with Chic and gave the hotel a thorough going-over. On the way back Chic declared that he was definitely going ahead with the purchase. There would be a disco every Friday and Saturday and he would erect a big sign above the door, proclaiming it to be 'Chic Murray's Hotel (Prop: Chic Murray)'. Signs would also be put up on the main roads for miles around pointing the way.

Bernie tried in vain to explain what a nightmare all this would be to organize – that planning permission alone would be a minefield. And at the end of the day, he added, who was going to beat a path to Coldstream? Nothing he could say, however, could dampen Chic's enthusiasm.

Two days later Chic phoned Bernie and asked to meet him for lunch. Naturally Bernie asked, as soon as they met, what stage the negotiations for the hotel had reached. 'What hotel?' Chic replied, with one of his blank stares. 'Get the drinks set up, Bernie.' The word 'hotel' was never mentioned again. Chic had clearly moved on, as was his wont, to another enthusiasm. 'Maybe I should open a chain of wishing wells,' he mused over coffee to his friend.

●

One day Chic arrived, soaking wet, at Jennie Wales's music department at the BBC. It had been raining for hours and even with his brolly and old raincoat he was absolutely 'platchin' '.

'I've got to get away,' he explained. 'This weather's terrible. I need a holiday. Can I use your phone to make the booking, Jennie?'

Seconds later he was dialling the number of the long-suffering travel agent. Jennie saw him looking bemused as the connection was made. Putting his hand over the mouthpiece, he explained to Jennie, 'Somehow I've got a crossed line. There's an old dear come on the telephone.'

His eyes lit up as he started to talk to the lady. 'Who are you?' she asked. Jennie watched as Chic rose to the challenge.

'Well, you know how it's been raining for hours?' he answered. 'I'm an angel forced down to earth because my wings are soaking wet!'

'Oh, *never*,' the old lady replied. 'Is *that so*?'

'It certainly is,' Chic blithely replied. 'I've got to wait here on earth until they dry off and I thought I'd have a wee chat with you first and fill in the time.'

'Mercy me. Hold on, Mr Angel. I can hardly believe my ears. Just a minute, I'll get my siser, Mary. She's got to hear this!'

Chic heard the sister being called and got Jennie to pick up the extension phone to listen while he filled her in on what had happened. They both heard the old lady call, 'Mary! Hurry to the phone this minute. There's an angel on the line talking to us. His wings got wet and he's having to stay down here until they're dried. Imagine!'

Jennie looked at the gleeful Chic, utterly in his element.

'Hello,' he said, 'is that you, Mary? Terrible thing to happen to a wee angel, don't you think?'

Mary replied, 'Are you *really* an angel? I thought Bella was having me on. How do we know you're an angel? And what's it like in heaven?'

At that moment another phone in Jennie's office rang. 'What's that ringing noise?' Mary asked excitedly.

'Hold on a minute,' said Chic, 'I'll need to answer it. Gosh, what a busy wee angel I am this morning.'

A few seconds later he was back. 'Hello, Mary and Bella,' he said, 'do I need to tell you who that was on the other phone for me?'

A sharp intake of breath was followed by the sound of the two sisters in animated conversation.

'Hello, hello,' said Chic. 'Look dears, I've got to go now. *He* says so and the wings are dry enough now. I'll need to do a wee trial run first and see if I can get off the ground, but I think I'll be able to make it.'

'Cheerio, Mr Angel,' Chic and Jennie heard the two sisters say. 'We hope you get back up all right.'

'I enjoyed our wee chat,' Chic replied. 'Ta-ta for now.'

It occurred to Jennie that Chic's description of himself as a grounded angel was not so far off the mark.

31

TRIBUTES TO A UNIQUE COMIC GENIUS

JIMMY REID

Chic's technique was to make sensible remarks about a screwball world and be viewed as a lovable screwball. His humour was surrealist, in the same class as that marvellous American funnyman, George Burns – The Best.

•

SPIKE MILLIGAN

He was one of the top comics in the world.

•

JUDI DENCH

I remember Chic in Bangkok when we made the film, *Saigon, Year of the Cat*, together. He insisted on calling me Judith – a name I have never been known by except when people were cross with me at school!

Chic was totally unique to me because he could tell me a story at enormous length, of which I would probably only catch five words, but he would make me laugh until the tears poured down my face.

In Bangkok, on days off, I have a vivid picture

of Chic lying in the hottest sun one can possibly imagine – in fact, during the filming he was known as the 'old leather bag'.

I was thrilled to have had the opportunity to know him and to work with him. Chic was truly unique.

•

ROY HUDD
Chic Murray – the Scottish W.C. Fields. A one off!

•

RONNIE BARKER
Chic Murray was a truly original comedian. I was much influenced by his wry way with words, and I also used his voice, or rather my version of it, for many years in *The Navy Lark* on radio, as Lieutenant Queeg, the engineer. I loved his work.

•

ERIC SYKES
One of the all-time greats – a Scottish W.C. Fields.

•

BILLY CONNOLLY
Chic was the master funny man – a genius. I hope as time goes by I can hone my material as fine as Chic. He goes into his tales like a story and *becomes* all the characters. That's what I ideally aspire to as a comedian – to be as good as him. I'd like to get more off the wall as I get older, the way he has done.

•

ROBBIE COLTRANE
He ranks with Tommy Cooper as the comedian all comedians call 'the boss'.

W. GORDON SMITH

There was something essentially sad and forlorn about Chic that reminded you of Jacques Tati. They both looked as if they'd lived out of carrier bags most of their lives. His comedy was, quite simply, unique. In France they would have made him an international film star. In America a Manhattan night club would have offered him their celebrity spot for life. In Italy there would have been a spaghetti named after him.

•

RIKKI FULTON

Rikki Fulton recalls how Chic used to single him out in company for 'the treatment', for he knew that he sent Rikki into fits. 'Yet there was always that edge of uncertainty with Chic. You might be talking to him in the street – and there always existed the possibility that somehow or other he would say or do something totally outrageous. When the pennies dropped with Chic, though, they were often pure gold.

•

JACK MILROY

'He'll always be remembered,' says Rikki's partner Jack Milroy, the other half of the *Francie and Josie* team. 'He'd walk on stage in evening dress and bunnet and everyone would say, "*Aw*, there's Big Chic".'

•

IAN CHRISTIE

BBC producer Ian Christie describes him as living on a magic carpet floating above everybody else.

'He had to use the facilities of this world, like four wheels or a bed, but then he was off again. He came into your life like a wee bird coming in through the window. You were allocated so much time, then he flew away again.'

•

HAROLD HOBSON

When actor Alex Norton referred to Chic as a 'verbal Picasso' he was adding to the list of references over the years that began with *Sunday Times*' critic Harold Hobson and his comparisons to Proust and Beckett.

'I thought the Scottish comedian Chic Murray first-rate,' Hobson wrote of Chic's 1956 West End début at the Prince of Wales Theatre. 'His dissection of the process of getting up in the morning is Proustian in its detail, Beckettish in its innumerable qualifications and wholly his own in its irresistible delight.'

•

To Jennie Wales at the BBC, however, Chic will always be the grounded angel with soaking wet wings, waiting for them to dry so he could take off again.